D0188517

The Lake District

AA Publishing

Produced by AA Publishing

© The Automobile Association 1997
Maps © The Automobile Association 1997

First published 1997

Published by AA Publishing (a trading name of Automobile Association Developments Limited, whose registered office is Norfolk House, Priestley Road, Basingstoke, Hampshire RG24 9NY; registered number 1878835).

ISBN 0 7495 1494 9

A CIP catalogue record for this book is available from the British Library.

The contents of this book are believed correct at the time of printing. Neverthless, the publishers cannot be held responsible for any errors or omissions or for changes in the details given in this book or for the consequences of any reliance on the information provided by the same. Material in this book has been previously published by AA Publishing in various publications.

AA Publishing would like to thank Roland Smith, Head of Information Services for The Peak National Park and Chairman of The Outdoor Writers' Guild, for his feature 'The Lake District'.

Colour separation by BTB, Digital Imaging, Whitchurch, Hampshire

Printed and bound by George Over Ltd, Rugby

THE LAKE DISTRICT

The Lake District National Park is Britain's largest, its 885 square miles (2,292sq km) consisting mostly of moorland and fell. Formed from glacial meltwater, the 16 lakes, of which Windermere is the largest, are arranged like spokes of a wheel in the mountain valleys and they reflect the highest peaks in England – Scafell Pike, Scafell, Skiddaw, Helvellyn, the Langdale Pikes and many more – in a magical clarity and quality of light.

Around Skiddaw and in the south of the park are angular and rounded hills, while the central area, including Scafell Pike, is wild and rugged country. Crowded in summer, Windermere and Ambleside are boating and touring centres. Grasmere and Rydal, noted for their Wordsworth associations, and Coniston for John Ruskin, are finely situated. Environmentally sensitive electric boats can be hired from the National Park Boating Centre at Coniston. Keswick, on Derwent Water, is a centre for walkers and holidaymakers alike, and a focal point for the northern lakes.

Neolithic stone circles such as Castlerigg, and Roman forts such as Hardknott, reflect Lakeland's long history. Former iron workings and more modern slate-quarrying have also left their mark on the landscape. Townend at Troutbeck is a fine example of a 17th-century local yeoman farmer's house. The National Trust, the biggest landowner within the National Park, looks after some of the finest landscapes for the enjoyment of future generations. The Forestry Commission and North West Water are other major landowners, but most of the land is in the care of farmers and estates.

The 1,800 miles (2,896km) of public paths provide unrivalled walking and climbing, from gentle lakeside strolls to testing mountain ascents.

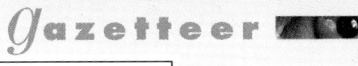
Situated on the western shores of Ullswater, on National Trust land, the series of splendid waterfalls are known by the name of the largest. The spectacular 70-ft (21-m) drop of Aira Force tumbles down the wooded ravine, and there are views of the waters from nearby footbridges.

AIRA FORCE
*WATERFALL IN AIRA BECK,
NEAR DOCKRAY*

Set on the northern edge of lake Windermere, and a convenient base for touring the central Lakes, Ambleside is a popular tourist centre. Tiny Bridge House, perched on the old packhorse bridge over Stock Ghyll, once housed a family with six children and is now a National Trust information centre.

Ambleside's literary associations include William Wordsworth who had his office here when he was Distributor of Stamps for Westmorland. St Mary's Church has a mural depicting the annual rushbearing ceremony when children walk through the town carrying rushes which are laid in the church. The ceremony, which originates from medieval times, is held on the first Saturday in July. The town is also the venue for the traditional Lakeland sports of hound trails, fell racing and Cumberland and Westmorland wrestling, held on the Thursday before the first Monday in August.

AMBLESIDE
*SMALL TOWN ON A591,
4 MILES (6.5KM) NW OF
WINDERMERE*

The former county town of Westmorland stands in a loop of the tree-lined River Eden and is dominated by Appleby Castle, a mainly 17th-century building with an impressive 11th-century keep. The Appleby Horse Fair, the largest gypsy gathering in Britain, is 300 years old and takes place in June. One of the oldest organs in Britain, moved here from Carlisle Cathedral, is housed in the Church of St Lawrence. The redoubtable Lady Anne Clifford, who restored several buildings in the town, is buried here.

The grounds of beautifully preserved Appleby Castle provide a natural setting for a farm park featuring rare breeds of British farm animals and also a large collection of ornamental waterfowl and unusual birds. The fine Norman keep and the Great Hall of the house are open to the public. The buildings in the old stable courtyard provide a display area for the Made in Cumbria exhibition, featuring work of the highly skilled craftspeople of the area.

APPLEBY-IN-WESTMORLAND
*SMALL TOWN OFF A66,
12 MILES (19KM) SE OF
PENRITH*

Barrow, on the Furness Peninsula, is a 19th-century industrial town with long, narrow streets of terraced houses around a busy centre. The Dock Museum on North Road tells the story of Barrow's maritime traditions. North-east of the town, in the beautiful 'Glen of Deadly Nightshade' is Furness Abbey (English Heritage). Built in 1157, the extensive remains of the church and other buildings are a reminder that this was once a very wealthy Cistercian establishment.

BARROW-IN-FURNESS
*TOWN ON A590, 18 MILES
(29KM) NW OF LANCASTER*

A silver birch cascades with autumn colour above the shores of Derwent Water in Borrowdale

BASSENTHWAITE
VILLAGE OFF A591, 6 MILES (9.5KM) N OF KESWICK

The village is located near the lake of same name, and has remains left behind by ancient Britons and the Romans. It lies to the north-east of Bassenthwaite Lake which, at 4 miles (6.5km) long, is the fourth largest lake in the National Park. The Norman Church of St Bega is near by.

BOOT
HAMLET OFF A595, 6 MILES (9.5KM) NE OF RAVENGLASS

At the Eskdale end of the Ravenglass and Eskdale Railway, Boot is a tiny village with a pub, the Woolpack, which was a resting place for packhorses transporting fleeces to the coast. Boot also marks the beginning of the climb up Hardknott Pass.

BORROWDALE
VALLEY OF RIVER DERWENT, S OF DERWENT WATER

Often considered the prettiest valley in the Lake District, it stretches south from the head of Derwent Water to Seathwaite, the starting point of many fell walks and rock climbing forays. The B5289 from Keswick

runs along most of its length, passing Derwent Water and National Trust woodland south of Grange. The Allerdale Ramble is a 58-mile (93-km) walk from Borrowdale valley to Silloth.

A pretty village on a hill, with a village green next to an old coaching inn, the White Hart.

BOUTH
VILLAGE OFF A590, 5 *MILES* *(8KM)* NE *OF* ULVERSTON

A busy tourist town on the edge of Windermere, which developed when the railway line opened, as it was the nearest accessible point on the lake. Most of the lake cruisers operate from here on the 10-mile

BOWNESS-ON-WINDERMERE
SUBURB ON A592, *IMMEDIATELY* S *OF* WINDERMERE

(16-km) stretch of Windermere. Just a short stroll from the lake, at the bottom of Bowness Hill, is the Old Laundry which features exhibitions and events and also houses the World of Beatrix Potter – a popular tourist attraction which brings to life the stories of Peter Rabbit and Jemima Puddleduck and other well-loved characters.

Wooden launches of a bygone era share moorings with more modern craft at the lakeside

The village lies at the foot of the Whinlatter Pass surrounded by mountains, and was formerly the seat of the woollen industry. There is a picnic site just outside the village.

BRAITHWAITE
VILLAGE ON B5292, 2 *MILES* *(3KM)* W *OF* KESWICK

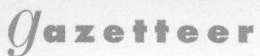

BROCKHOLE, THE LAKE DISTRICT NATIONAL PARK VISITOR CENTRE
On A591, 2 miles (3km) NW of Windermere
Tel: 015394 46601

Brockhole, built in 1899 for a wealthy businessman, is a large house, set in 32 acres (13ha) of landscaped gardens and grounds, standing on the eastern shore of lake Windermere. In 1969 it became England's first National Park Visitor Centre. Operated by the Lake District National Park Authority its purpose is to help visitors to enjoy and appreciate England's largest National Park. The Centre offers exhibitions, audio-visual programmes, lake cruises, an exciting adventure playground and an extensive events programme.

Open Apr–Oct, daily. Grounds and gardens only open all year.

BROTHERS WATER
Lake off A592, 3 miles (5km) N of Kirkstone Pass

Situated at the foot of Kirkstone Pass, this is one of the smallest of the lakes. It is shown as 'Broad Water' on old maps; the name may have changed after two brothers fell through the ice and drowned.

BROUGHAM CASTLE
At Brougham village, 2 miles (3km) SE of Penrith, on minor road off A66
Tel: 01768 62488

The restoration of Brougham, and of the nearby Appleby and Brough castles, is chiefly the work of the immensely rich and powerful Anne Clifford, Countess of Dorset, Pembroke and Montgomery. She wanted all of her castles to be habitable, and spent large sums of money making them so. She died at Brougham Castle in 1678 when she was almost 90 years old.

Brougham's origins date back to the time of Henry II when – probably around 1170 – the great tower was built. It was made of sandstone rubble, with more expensive, decorative cut stone at the corners and on windows and doors. The tower had buttresses on three walls, and a forebuilding on the fourth wall. It seems that the tower was originally intended to have only three storeys, but a fourth floor was added later. This later work is of a much better quality than the original, a difference that can be clearly distinguished today. Other buildings were added to the keep, most notably in the 17th century by Anne Clifford. However, the splendid great tower remains Brougham's most impressive feature, still standing almost to its original height. There is an exhibition of Roman tombstones from the nearby fort. Brougham Castle is in the care of English Heritage.

(See also Cycle ride: Penrith and Northern Lakeland, page 62.)

Open Apr–Oct, daily.

BROUGHTON-IN-FURNESS
Village on A593, 8 miles (13km) NW of Ulverston

On the southern edge of the National Park, this market town lies close to where the River Duddon flows into the sea. The name derives from the old English word meaning

'stronghold'. It was of strategic importance through centuries of invasion from Scotland and overseas.

Surrounded by high fells, this popular beauty spot lies between lake Buttermere and Crummock Water. The village is connected with a great 19th-century scandal, when Mary Robinson, the 'Beauty of Buttermere', thought she had married the Earl of Hopetoun's brother only to discover later that her husband was a bankrupt impostor. He was later hanged.

The lake is separated from neighbouring Crummock Water by a narrow strip of meadowland. Most of the land around Buttermere is owned by the National Trust and there is an easy 5-mile (8-km) walk around the lake with stunning views to enjoy in all directions.

BUTTERMERE
HAMLET AND LAKE ON B5289, 8 MILES (13KM) SW OF KESWICK

The shores of Buttermere can be explored on foot

CALDBECK
VILLAGE ON B5299, 7 MILES (11KM) SE OF WIGTON

The name means 'cold brook' and water was once harnessed to drive a variety of mills for grinding corn and weaving. John Peel is buried in the churchyard where his tombstone bears a carved hunting horn. Mary Robinson, the 'Beauty of Buttermere', is also buried here. The old brewery, which once supplied 16 inns in the village, is still standing.

CALDER BRIDGE
VILLAGE ON A595, 4 MILES (6.5KM) SE OF EGREMONT

Originally this was an agricultural community but it is now a residential village for workers at the Sellafield Nuclear Power Station. The power station's visitor centre explains the working of the nuclear power industry. Calder Abbey, just outside the village, was founded as a Cistercian abbey. It is now a ruin.

CARTMEL
VILLAGE OFF A590, 4 MILES (6.5KM) S OF NEWBY BRIDGE

Cartmel is an ancient and lovely place, sited in the middle of a peninsula that juts out on to the sands of Morecambe Bay. The great priory pervades its every corner. The Church of St Mary and St Michael dates from the founding of the Augustinian priory by William Marshall at the end of the 12th century and, unusually, survived the Dissolution intact, remaining in use as the parish church. Inside are massive columns, a vast east window and some wonderful carving (do not miss the exquisite misericords). Externally, the diagonally-set tower dwarfs the houses of the village at its feet. The only other remnant of the priory complex is its gatehouse in the small cobbled square. The one large room over the archway was used as a lock-up and then in the 17th and 18th centuries as a school, and it is now in the care of

The beautiful 12th-century priory church at Cartmel

the National Trust. Cottages and shops of stone or traditional roughcast, sometimes painted, make attractive groupings around the square and in the streets that lead off it. Many houses were constructed using stone from the demolished priory buildings. One street runs down to the little River Eea, another out past the racecourse where meetings are held on bank holiday weekends. Legend has it that the monks started Cartmel Races as their Whitsun recreation.

This ancient market town stands on the edge of the National Park, at the confluence of the River Cocker and the River Derwent. Cockermouth has a printing museum, a toy and model museum, an art gallery and Jennings' Brewery which operates guided tours. Sheepdog trials are held here in late May, and the agricultural show in early August has the traditional Lakeland sports of hound trails and Cumberland and Westmorland wrestling.

(See also Cycle ride: The Cockermouth Circuit, page 12.)

William Wordsworth was born here in Cockermouth on 7 April 1770, and happy memories of the house had a great effect on his work. He played on the garden terrace with his sister Dorothy, and the inside staircase panelling and other features are original. Portraits and other items connected with the poet are displayed. Wordsworth House is owned by the National Trust.
Open Apr–Oct, most days.

COCKERMOUTH
Town off A66, 8 miles (13km) E of Workington

Wordsworth House
Main St
Tel: 01900 824805

THE COCKERMOUTH CIRCUIT

This route explores quiet lanes around the fringes of the Lake District before entering the National Park at Waterend. There are excellent views from the smooth round hills of the north, to the rugged, volcanic, central mountains of the Helvellyn and Scafell ranges. Approaching Loweswater there are spectacular views into the heart of the mountains. There is one steep hill, otherwise the terrain offers surprisingly easy cycling.

INFORMATION

Total Distance
23 miles (37km)

Difficulty
Moderate

OS Maps
Landranger 1:50,000 sheet 89 (West Cumbria)

Tourist Information
Cockermouth,
tel: 01900 822634

Cycle Shops/Hire
Derwent Cycles, Cockermouth,
tel: 01900 822113;
Track & Trail Mountain Bikes,
Cockermouth,
tel: 01900 827243

Nearest Railway Station
Workington (6 miles/9.5km)

Refreshments
There are several pubs and cafés in Cockermouth. On the route is Grange Country House Hotel at Waterend serving coffee, tea and meals. A good place for lunch is Kirkstile Inn, Loweswater; there are also pubs at Eaglesfield, Dean and Lorton and a village shop at Lorton. The route includes several suitable spots for picnics.

The Earl of Mayo's statue in Cockermouth is the starting point of the ride

Cycle ride

START

Cockermouth lies just north of the A66, between the A595 and A5086. There are several car parks, including near the Tourist Information Centre, off Market Place. The ride begins in Main Street (parking, toilets) at the statue of the Earl of Mayo.

DIRECTIONS

1. Go west along Main Street and turn left opposite Wordsworth House, signed 'A5086 Egremont'. After 110yds (100m), ignoring the 'no through road' sign, turn right into the continuation of Sullart Street, go uphill to the end, take the footpath straight ahead (not the cycle path on the right) and walk for 55yds (50m) to emerge at Fitz Road. Turn right here and go down the road for 450yds (400m); turn left before the stone arch, into Mayo Street. At the T-junction turn right (no signpost). Follow this road (ignoring 'no through road' sign) go through the gate, cross the A66 with care and follow the Brigham sign to Brigham.

2. In the centre of Brigham village, at the Apple Tree Inn, take the left fork, signed 'Eaglesfield', and soon turn left into Hotchberry Lane. Climb the hill, enjoying good views of the Lakeland mountains, and descend into Eaglesfield. To explore the village turn left just past the village sign. John Dalton's House is at the end of this lane. Return to the

Wordsworth House, Cockermouth

Deanscales Road to continue on the main route.

3. Continue on this lane to Deanscales and, as the road bends left, turn right, signed 'Dean/Braithwaite', and proceed to the T-junction. To visit St Oswald's Church continue over the crossroads to see the church facing you. Otherwise, turn left, signed 'Mockerkin/Loweswater'. Shortly after entering Dean turn right, signed 'Ullock/Lamplugh', and soon enter Ullock.

4. At the end of the green turn left, signposted 'Lamplugh/Loweswater'. Cross the beck after ½ mile (1km), then cross the A5096 with care by turning right then left, signposted 'Mockerkin/ Loweswater'. Climb steeply through Mockerkin, pausing at Mockerkin Howe at the top to rest and enjoy the expansive views from the west coast to the mountains in the east and south. Descend for ½ mile (1km), taking the next left turn,

signed 'Loweswater Lake'. Continue the steep descent, stopping partway for views of Loweswater and beyond.

5. At the bottom of the hill pass the Grange Country House Hotel. (From this point you may take a track on the right along the south side of the lake for 2 miles (3km) to Loweswater.) Continue on the main route, passing Waterend Farm and as you ride towards Loweswater see the steep-sided Mellbreak immediately ahead. Shortly arrive at a left turn; signed 'Thackthwaite', and take this route along Lorton Vale. (To visit the hamlet of Loweswater, continue past this junction for 220yds (200m) and turn right, signed 'Kirkstile Inn'.)

6. From the junction signed 'Thackthwaite' follow the gently undulating lane for 3½ miles (5.5km), through Thackthwaite to a T-junction where you turn left,

THE COCKERMOUTH CIRCUIT

signed 'Rogerscale'. (To explore Low Lorton/High Lorton turn right following the signs.)

7. Continue on this road for 2 miles (3km) and at a T-junction turn right, signed 'Embleton/Keswick'. Continue downhill, crossing the bridge over the River Cocker to a T-junction

with the B5292, and continue straight on, signed 'Embleton/Wythop'. In 1 mile (1.5km) turn left, signed 'Cockermouth', and continue, crossing the bridge over the A66. At the next T-junction turn right on to the B5292, descend into Cockermouth and follow the signs back to the town centre.

PLACES OF INTEREST

Cockermouth

This ancient market town standing at the confluence of the rivers Cocker and Derwent has plenty to interest the visitor. At one end of wide tree-lined Main Street is the castle in which Mary, Queen of Scots once took refuge. At the

WHAT TO LOOK OUT FOR

The roadside verges, ideal habitats for insects and wildlife, are abundant with seasonal flowers. Watch for buzzards, kestrel, wagtails, curlew, lapwings and many hedgerow birds as well as red squirrel. Hill farming, dry-stone walls, moorland scenery and wetlands are all a feature of this area.

Dean

St Oswald's Church, dating from the 12th century with later chancel and sanctuary, lies picturesquely on the edge of the village. The interior includes renovated oak pews and pulpits bearing the carved mark of the famous 'mouse man', Robert Thompson. Other features of interest include the gargoyles, ancient gravestones and the preaching cross, which is 12th-century or earlier.

Loweswater

One of the Lake District's smaller lakes, Loweswater claims to be the only lake to flow inland, draining into Crummock Water. Sheep graze on the surrounding woodland and meadow, and the woods administered by the National Trust, are traversed by many leafy paths.

(See also page 56.)

Preparing lunch in Wordsworth House, Cockermouth

Lush hills around Loweswater

other end is Wordsworth House.
(See also page 11.)

Eaglesfield

This village was the birthplace of John Dalton (1766-1844), a great chemist and discoverer of the atomic theory.

COLTON
HAMLET OFF A5092, 5 MILES (8KM) N OF ULVERSTON

The tiny hamlet comprises a handful of farms and cottages. Colton Old Hall was the seat of the Sandy family in the 17th century.

CONISTON
VILLAGE ON A593, 6 MILES (9.5KM) SW OF AMBLESIDE

The village is in a superb setting near the northern tip of Coniston Water overlooked by The Old Man of Coniston at 2,635ft (803m) high. Copper was first mined here by the Romans, and the industry and the village grew rapidly in the 18th and 19th centuries. The old mines were abandoned when copper was discovered elsewhere. A popular walk passes through Coppermines Valley.

Brantwood
2½ MILES (4KM) SE OF CONISTON ON AN UNCLASSIFIED ROAD OFF B5285 REGULAR FERRY SERVICES FROM CONISTON PIER
TEL: 015394 41396

Brantwood, the former home of John Ruskin, is one of the most beautifully situated houses in the Lake District with fine views across

Coniston Water. Inside there is a large collection of Ruskin paintings and other memorabilia, while outside visitors can enjoy delightful nature walks through the Brantwood Estate.

Open mid Mar–mid Nov, daily. Rest of year, most days.

Launched in 1859, the graceful *Gondola*, owned by the National Trust, worked on Coniston Water until 1937, and came back into service in 1980. Now visitors can once again enjoy her silent progress and old-fashioned comfort. The round trip takes about an hour.

Open Apr–Oct to scheduled daily timetable. Trips commence from Coniston Pier. Piers at Coniston, Park-a-Moor at SE end of lake and Brantwood. (Not National Trust.)

Steam Yacht *Gondola*
PIER COTTAGE
TEL: *015394 41288*

The graceful steam yacht Gondola plies a summertime route on Coniston Water

CONISTON WATER
LAKE OFF A593/B5285, 6 MILES (9.5KM) SW OF AMBLESIDE

The lake is 5 miles (8km) long and 180ft (55m) deep; a minor road runs between its eastern shore and the slopes of Grizedale Forest. The steam yacht *Gondola* leaves from Coniston on a round trip of the lake stopping at Park-a-Moor and Brantwood. Boats can be launched on the public slipway and there are sailing dinghies and windsurfers for hire. Powered craft are not allowed on the lake. In 1967 Donald Campbell was killed on Coniston Water when attempting to break the water speed record. A memorial plaque in Coniston records the details.

CROOK
VILLAGE ON B5284, 4 MILES (6.5KM) NW OF KENDAL

A pleasant Lakeland village midway between Kendal and Bowness-on-Windermere. The church has a bell dating from the 14th century.

CROSTHWAITE
HAMLET OFF A5074, 5 MILES (8KM) W OF KENDAL

The name means 'cross in a clearing' and it is thought that there has been a chapel or church here for centuries.

CRUMMOCK WATER
LAKE OFF B5289, NEXT TO BUTTERMERE

Crummock Water is separated from Buttermere lake by a narrow strip of meadowland. It is fed on its western side by Scale Force, the highest waterfall in the Lake District at 172ft (52m). Its ancient name was Cromack Water.

DACRE
VILLAGE OFF A592, 4 MILES (6.5KM) SW OF PENRITH

The village has a 14th-century castle which belonged to one of the great northern families until the 16th century. The Norman church stands on the site of a Saxon monastery. In the churchyard are four

Crummock Water, one of the chain that includes Loweswater and Buttermere

stones each depicting a bear – one is asleep, one is being attacked by a cat, another is grabbing the cat and the fourth bear is eating the cat. Nobody knows the meaning of the stones.

The stately home of Dalemain was originally a medieval pele tower, which was added to in Tudor times and later, with the imposing Georgian façade completed in 1745. It has splendid oak panelling, Chinese wallpaper, Tudor plasterwork and fine Queen Anne and Georgian furniture. The rooms include a Victorian nursery and a housekeeper's room. The tower contains the Westmorland and Cumberland Yeomanry Museum, and there is an interesting countryside museum in the 16th-century cobbled courtyard. The grounds include a deerpark and gardens, and there is an adventure playground.

Open Apr–Oct, most days.

Dalemain
NE OF DACRE ON A MINOR ROAD
TEL: 017684 86450

Derwent Water and the River Derwent from Surprise View at the southern end of the lake

DERWENT WATER
LAKE OFF B5289, SW OF KESWICK

The third largest lake in the Lake District, Derwent Water is also the widest at 1¼ miles (2km) and is dotted with islands. In the centre is St Herbert's Island, named after the saint who lived here as a hermit. Derwent Island was once home to German miners who worked near Keswick and in Newlands Valley. This popular lake can be explored by the boat from Keswick which stops at various landing stages, allowing visitors to take the many footpaths through the surrounding

woodland and up to different viewpoints. On the east side of Derwent Water is Friar's Crag, from where there is a famous view of the lake, considered by John Ruskin to be one of the finest views in Europe.

The River Duddon rises to the north-east of Hardknott Pass and flows south through the unspoilt scenery of Dunnerdale to the estuary of Duddon Sands.

DUNNERDALE
VALLEY OF RIVER DUDDON,
W OF A593

Walk

THE EDEN VALLEY

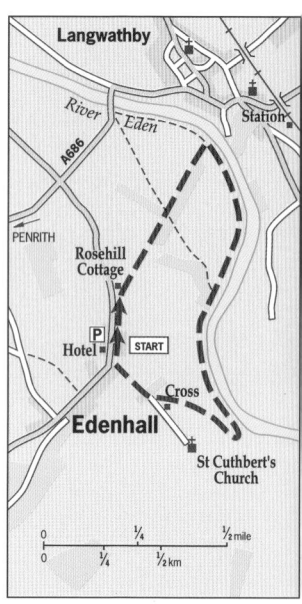

*T*he Eden Valley, between the Lake District and the North Pennines, is one of the most beautiful pastoral landscapes in Britain. The fact that it is often by-passed by visitors helps to maintain its unspoilt quality. This walk is a gentle introduction to the river and one of its most interesting villages.

Grid ref: NY565325

INFORMATION
The walk is about 2 miles (3km) long.
Generally very easy underfoot with one short incline.
A few gates and no stiles.
Some road walking in Edenhall, a quiet village with only light traffic.
The Edenhall Hotel provides bar meals and there is a play area.

START
Edenhall lies just off the A686, 2 miles (3km) south of Langwathby. Park either in the village or close to the Edenhall Hotel, from where the walk begins.

DIRECTIONS
Walk out of the village past the children's play area. Just before

The Plague Cross at Edenhall

the red-brick Rosehill Cottage turn right and go through the gate, signposted 'Langwathby and River Eden'. Walk along the track with a fence to your right and sheep pasture to your left. Ahead in the distance is the village of Langwathby. Continue to a wicket gate, between narrow conifer plantations, and keep forward along the path. On reaching the river turn right, signposted 'Edenhall and Church' and walk along the river bank on a raised path to go through a gate. Proceed uphill, past the end of the conifer plantation to your right, then follow a line of beech trees, with a steep slope and the river to your left. Continue along the path (which can be overgrown in summer), passing the high wall of the Edenhall estate deer park on your right, and go down some

steps to follow the edge of the park until the river veers away to your left. Go through a wicket gate to join a track, and bear sharp right to follow this over the parkland, past a lone oak and towards the stone Plague Cross. (Here you can detour to the left to see St Cuthbert's Church, retracing your steps to the cross.)

Bear right along the metalled track, past the East Lodge and into the village. Turn right on the main road to return to the start.

Edenhall

Edenhall is an estate village, created by the Musgrave and Gibson families. The hall itself no longer exists, but there are some beautiful buildings in soft red sandstone, characteristic of the Eden Valley. 'Homefield', close to the tall farmhouse, was a tithe barn and the church tower was once used as a pele, a refuge from raiding Scots at the time of the Border wars.

The Plague Cross

The stone cross towards the end of the walk is called the Plague Cross and dates back to four hundred years ago, when an

St Cuthbert's Church, Edenhall

epidemic struck the village and killed a quarter of its inhabitants. As no tradesman would risk entering the stricken village or make any kind of contact with its people, villagers paid for their food by placing money in a sink of vinegar beneath the cross.

WHAT TO LOOK OUT FOR

Otters still inhabit the Eden, although they are rarely seen. Most daytime sightings are cases of mistaken identity, usually referring to mink which have become quite common here over the last decade. Birds of the river include goosander and cormorant during spring and summer; dippers and grey wagtails are residents and kingfishers come and go. In winter, skeins of greylag geese fly up and down the valley, filling the air with their contact calls.

EGREMONT
*SMALL TOWN OFF A595,
5 MILES (8KM) SE OF
WHITEHAVEN*

A small market town with an annual crab apple celebration dating from the 13th century and featuring the World Gurning Championship. Wordsworth's poem 'The Horn of Egremont Castle' is based on a local medieval legend, whereby a great horn hanging in the castle can only be blown by the rightful lord. In this instance the impostor flees to a monastery. Lowes Court Gallery on Main Street dates from the 16th century and promotes local arts and crafts.

ELTERWATER
*VILLAGE ON B5343, 3 MILES
(5KM) W OF AMBLESIDE*

An unspoilt village and smallest of the lakes, surrounded by volcanic crags and waterfalls. The name means 'swan lake' in Norse; migrating whooper swans can be seen on the lake in winter.

Main picture: The shores of Ennerdale Water are best explored on foot
Left: Visitors throng the streets of Egremont during the Crab Apple Fair

In a remote corner of the Lake District, Ennerdale Water is a reservoir serving Cumbria. Its shores are best explored on foot as access by car is limited. A path leads east from the car park at Bowness Knot along the northern shore of the lake. Both the lake and the nearby village of Ennerdale Bridge take their name from the River Ehen.

A beautiful valley approached from the east through the steep Wrynose and Hardknott Passes. The Ravenglass and Eskdale Railway, which once carried ore from the Eskdale mines to the coast, now carries holidaymakers and walkers into this fine walking country.

A small lake, surrounded by farmland and situated between Windermere and Coniston Water. Esthwaite Water is usually first sited after passing through Far and Near Sawrey on the way to Hawkshead.

A lime kiln by the church in this farming village was used until 1922 for producing quicklime. Coppices were also grown here for charcoal-burning.

ENNERDALE WATER
LAKE OFF A5086, 1 MILE (1.5KM) E OF ENNERDALE BRIDGE

ESKDALE
VALLEY W OF HARDKNOTT PASS

ESTHWAITE WATER
LAKE OFF B5258, S OF HAWKSHEAD

FIELD BROUGHTON
HAMLET OFF A590, 2 MILES (3KM) N OF CARTMEL

FINSTHWAITE
HAMLET OFF A590, 1 MILE (1.5KM) N OF NEWBY BRIDGE

The village can trace its history back to Viking times. The extensive surrounding woodlands of oak, birch and hazel have been cut and used in the furniture and building trades. The Stott Park Bobbin Mill was opened in 1835 to make bobbins for the growing textile industry.

FURNESS
HISTORIC REGION IN NW ENGLAND

This peninsula in south Lakeland owes much of its economic development to the methodical exploitation of all natural resources by the monks of Furness Abbey.

GLENRIDDING
VILLAGE ON A592, 1 MILE (1.5KM) NW OF PATTERDALE

The village lies at the foot of the Kirkstone Pass as the road descends into the valley towards Ullswater. It is also at the start of the Helvellyn Ridge Walk.

(See also Walk: Discovering Ullswater, page 82.)

GOSFORTH
VILLAGE OFF A595, 5 MILES (8KM) NW OF RAVENGLASS

Gosforth cross, the tallest sandstone monolith in Britain, is carved with both Norse and Christian symbols. There is also a Viking 'fishing stone' and Viking carved stones are built into a toolshed, now a Listed building. The oldest building dates back to 1628, and now houses the library and supper room.

GRANGE
HAMLET ON B5289, 5 MILES (8KM) S OF KESWICK

The village lies just outside Borrowdale at the head of Derwent Water. A great double-arched bridge stretches more than 100yds (91.5m) over the River Derwent. Castle Crag (National Trust) is a famous viewpoint at the Jaws of Borrowdale. Grange Fell includes the hill King's How, 1,363ft (415m), and the Bowder Stone, a huge Ice Age granite mass.

GRANGE-OVER-SANDS
SMALL TOWN ON B5277, 2 MILES (3KM) SE OF CARTMEL

The little grey town, more a retirement community than a resort today, has its back to the Lake District and looks south over a magnificent prospect of the alluring and treacherous sands of Morecambe Bay. Once known, somewhat flatteringly, as 'Cumbria's Riviera', it has a sheltered site, a gentle climate, pleasant 19th-century hotels, and attractive gardens planted with exotic shrubs. The 'grange' in the town's name belonged to the monks of medieval Cartmel Priory, who had a vineyard here and a small harbour for bringing in sea coal. As a resort, Grange was boosted by the railway from Furness, which arrived in 1857 and in characteristic

Victorian style was built unhesitatingly along the seafront, between the village and the shore. The promenade along the front was built in 1904.

A fashionable health spa developed on the strength of the water from St Ann's Well at Humphrey Head, a limestone headland 3 miles (5km) to the south, which was good for gout. There is a pleasant walk to Humphrey Head, where England's last wolf is said to have been killed (though it has been sardonically suggested that it must have gone to Grange to retire). Another enjoyable walk leads over Hampsfield Fell to Cartmel, with its impressive priory church.

Grange-over-Sands lies on the north shore of Morecambe Bay

GRASMERE

VILLAGE OFF A591, 3 MILES (5KM) NW OF AMBLESIDE

Purplish grey-green houses tucked into the wooded lower slopes of Lakeland's grassy hills – in William Wordsworth's words, 'the loveliest spot the man hath ever found'. Grasmere would surely find a place in every guidebook on its own merits, but it is for its associations with Wordsworth and his family that it is best known.

The moon was up, the Lake was shining clear
Among the hoary mountains; from the shore
I push'd, and struck the oars and struck again
In cadence, and my little boat moved on...
Leaving behind her still on either side
Small circles glittering idly in the moon,
Until they melted all into one track
Of sparkling light.

The Prelude (1805)

Old cottages and shops, Victorian villas and guesthouses, galleries and hotels line the twisty main street. To the east the River Rothay winds down the back of the village to Grasmere lake, passing St Oswald's Church on its way. The church is faced with pebbledash outside but parts date from the 14th century at least. It was described by Wordsworth as:

...large and massy; for duration built;
With pillars crowded, and the roof upheld
By naked rafters intricately crossed
Like leafless underboughs in some thick wood,
All withered by the depth of shade above.

The Prelude

The roof structure is indeed interesting. The floor used to be of beaten earth and once a year would be covered with rushes gathered by the children of the village. Now it is flagged, but the Rushbearing Festival is still celebrated here each August. In the graveyard, near a yew planted by the poet, are the tombs of William Wordsworth, his wife, sister and other members of his family. Near the lych-gate is a small building which was once the school, where Wordsworth taught, and which since 1854 has been the home of Sarah Nelson's Celebrated Grasmere Gingerbread shop. The Grasmere Sports, first held in 1852, take place in August. Events include fell racing, hound trailing and Cumberland and Westmorland wrestling.

Above: The tranquil waters of Grasmere
Left: Dove Cottage, where Wordsworth wrote much of his finest romantic poetry

Wordsworth lived at Dove Cottage from 1799 to 1808, and during that time wrote much of his best-known poetry. The house is kept in its original condition, as described in the journals of his sister Dorothy, and the award-winning museum displays manuscripts, paintings and various items associated with the poet. Near the cottage is the former schoolroom where he taught, and Wordsworth, his wife and sister, and other members of the family, are buried in the churchyard. Residential courses are held by the Wordsworth Trust.

Open daily. Closed most of Jan, beginning of Feb & 24–26 Dec.

Dove Cottage & The Wordsworth Museum
S OF GRASMERE, OFF A591
TEL: 015394 35544 & 35547

29

WORDSWORTH AND THE LITERARY LANDSCAPE

Wordsworth

The poet Wordsworth was a prime mover in both the early popularisation and the preservation of the Lake District, and for many visitors the region is inseparable from the images created by Wordsworth and his fellow Lake Poets of the Romantic Age, Coleridge and Southey. Others came here to see the countryside portrayed in such minute and beautiful detail by the children's author Beatrix Potter, who lived for many years at Hill Top, Near Sawrey. The Tower Bank Arms, adjacent to Hill Top, featured in The Tale of Jemima Puddleduck *and Esthwaite Water was the home of Jeremy Fisher. Visitors also came to discover the land of adventure which featured in the stories of Arthur Ransome. More recently, the Lake District has appeared as the setting for popular novels by Richard Adams and Melvyn Bragg.*

Yet William Wordsworth, who was born and brought up in the market town of Cockermouth, in the north-western corner of the National Park, is still the linchpin of literary Lakeland. His early experiences of nature and the land around him – so vividly recalled in The Prelude, *perhaps his greatest work – influenced his writing throughout his long life (born in 1770, he died in 1850). Working with Samuel Taylor Coleridge, he developed a new style of poetry, considered accesible*

The kitchen parlour at Dove Cottage

to all, with which to communicate his ideas about man and nature and their influences upon each other. Wordsworth attended school at Hawkshead (where he carved his initials into one of the old wooden desks), and in 1799 settled with his devoted sister Dorothy at Dove Cottage in Grasmere, where they were to live for nine years. During this time Dorothy started her famous Grasmere journal, and her close and lively observations of nature proved a strong influence on both her brother and Coleridge, a frequent visitor. After William's marriage, the family eventually moved to Rydal Mount, and both homes are open to visitors. The family is buried together in the churchyard at Grasmere.

The Wordsworths and their writing attracted many other famous authors to the Lake District, which became a hive of literary activity,

perceived all at once as a desirable place to live in and visit – authors such as Sir Walter Scott, Charlotte Brontë and John Keats included the Lakes in their tours of the country, and John Ruskin, the celebrated Victorian critic of art, architecture and society made his home at Brantwood, on the shores of Coniston Water. Brantwood, which contains a large collection of his drawings and paintings, is open to visitors.

Ruskin

GREAT GABLE
Mountain 2 miles (3km)
NE of Wasdale Head

Popular with fell walkers, Great Gable (2,949ft/899m) can be approached from the south-west from Wast Water or from the north-east from Seathwaite Farm, passing the small bulk of Green Gable. At the top is a plaque recording the occasion when the area was given to the National Trust by the Fell and Rock Climbing Club as a memorial to their colleagues lost in World War I. A service is held here on Remembrance Sunday. The modern sport of climbing developed in the area in the 19th century.

Grizedale Forest was the first Forestry Commission estate where special efforts were made to provide information and other facilities for visitors. The centre illustrates the story of Grizedale from wild wood to its present role as an area managed for timber, wildlife and recreation. There is a conservation tree nursery, and a number of waymarked walks can be followed, ranging from the 1-mile (1.5-km) Millwood Habitat Trail to the 9-mile (14.5-km) Silurian Way. Routes for cyclists are also provided, and there are woodland sculptures, observation hides, a play area and picnic sites. The area gives wonderful views, with the possibility of seeing some woodland red and roe deer.

Open all year daily.

(See also Cycle ride: Hawkshead and Windermere's Shores, page 35.)

GRIZEDALE FOREST PARK
Off B5285, 3 miles (5km) S of Hawkshead
Tel: 01229 860010

Left: A view of Great Gable from Kirk Fell
Below: One of the many exhibits on the Grizedale Forest sculpture trail

Dance and drama, classical and jazz music, variety and folk concerts have all been featured at this unique theatre. It was founded in 1969, with an emphasis on quality, and is open during the day for exhibitions. Also of interest is a long-distance Sculpture Trail with around 60 sculptures, and The Gallery in the Forest which houses art, sculpture and craft exhibitions. Other attractions include a painting studio, and a sculpture trail for the disabled.

Open all year, most days. Sculpture trails open all year, daily.

Theatre in the Forest
Tel: 01229 860291

HARDKNOTT PASS
MOUNTAIN PASS BETWEEN
ESKDALE GREEN AND SKELWITH
BRIDGE

This steep pass rises 1,000ft (305m) out of Eskdale in just over 1 mile (1.5km). It is single-track in places, with hairpin bends and a gradient of 1-in-4. The pass is best avoided at peak holiday times or in icy conditions.

Hardknott Castle Roman Fort
AT W END OF HARDKNOTT
PASS

On this astonishing site above Eskdale, the Romans built a walled and ramparted fort covering nearly 3 acres (1ha), with a bathhouse and parade ground outside. The remains of the building can be seen.

Open any reasonable time. Access may be hazardous in winter.

HAVERTHWAITE
VILLAGE ON A590, 2 MILES
(3KM) SW OF NEWBY BRIDGE

The village lies on the River Leven. The Low Wood Gunpowder Works date from 1849; the gunpowder was removed, for safety reasons, by boat. Haverthwaite is the terminus of the Lakeside and Haverthwaite Railway.

(See also page 52.)

HAWESWATER
RESERVOIR OFF A590, W OF
SHAP

Haweswater was created in the 1930s by the Manchester Corporation to supply water to the industrial city, and beneath its surface lies the drowned village of Mardale. Wildlife flourishes in the area, with golden eagles and peregrine falcons breeding in the valley. Otters, roe and red deer and red squirrels also inhabit the area. A pleasant circular walk around Haweswater skirts the shore and passes through woodland.

HAWKSHEAD
VILLAGE ON B5285, 4 MILES
(6KM) S OF AMBLESIDE

It was not until the 19th century that there were roads to the village, and today's visitors park in the large car park to keep the maze of narrow streets and alleyways traffic free. Many of the buildings in the picturesque village date from the 17th century; the 15th-century parish church is set on a knoll overlooking the village. Wordsworth attended the grammar school here between 1779 and 1787 and lodged with Anne Tyson. Her cottage still stands and the grammar school, now a museum with an important antiquarian library, has Wordsworth's desk on which he carved his name.

(See also Cycle ride: Hawkshead and Windermere's Shores, page 35.)

Beatrix Potter Gallery
MAIN ST
Tel: 015394 36355

This exhibition of Beatrix Potter's original illustrations from her children's storybooks changes annually. Housed in the former office of her husband, solicitor William Heelis, the gallery is owned by the National Trust. There is also a display of her life as an author, artist, farmer and determined preserver of her beloved Lake District.

Open Apr—Oct, most days. Admission is by timed ticket including National Trust members.

*T*he ride takes in the lower hills of southern Cumbria, offering views of the high wild mountains, quiet cultivated valleys and fine examples of Lakeland farms and cottages. There are pleasantly demanding sections of rolling hills interspersed with level riding with the exception of two longer steep hills.

INFORMATION

Total Distance
21 miles (34km), with 3 miles (5km) off-road

Difficulty
Challenging

OS Map
Landranger 1:50,000 sheet 97 (Kendal to Morecambe)

Tourist Information
Hawkshead (summer only), tel: 015394 36525; Windermere, tel: 015394 46499

Cycle Shops/Hire
Ghyllside Cycles, Ambleside, tel: 015394 33592; Grizedale Mountain Bikes, tel: 01229 860369

Nearest Railway Station
Windermere

Refreshments
Hawkshead has many pubs and cafés; pubs on the route include The Eagle's Head at Satterthwaite, and there are tea rooms at the Grizedale Forest Visitor Centre. Grizedale Forest offers fine opportunities for picnicking.

The village of Hawkshead is associated with both William Wordsworth and Beatrix Potter

35

HAWKSHEAD AND WINDERMERE'S SHORES

Hanging baskets and colourful window boxes decorate the Queen's Head at Hawkshead

Continue for 2 miles (3km), passing through the village of Colthouse to reach High Wray. In High Wray, turn right at the junction, signed 'Ferry & Unsuitable for Vehicles'.

2. Continue past Balla Wray Nursing Home, passing through the woods of Claife Estate. After 1½ undulating miles (2.5km), at Red Nab go through the gate on to an unsurfaced road and ride along the lakeside, heading south. In 3 miles (5km) go over the cattle grid on to a tarmac road and eventually turn right on to the B5285.

3. After passing Ash Landing, climb the hill and immediately before the 'Far Sawrey' signpost turn left. Bear left again in a short distance, and descend to pass through High Cunsey. Follow this undulating lane for 2 miles (3km), bearing left at the fork in Low Cunsey: cross the stream and go over the hill to the T-junction opposite Graythwaite Hall.

4. Turn left here, and shortly right, signed 'Rusland'. Climb the hill and descend with care, then take the left fork to reach a junction by a telephone box, just after Crosslands Farm. Turn right, signed 'Grizedale', and follow

START

The village of Hawkshead lies midway between lake Windermere and Coniston Water on the B5285. It is 4 miles (6.5km) from the Windermere car ferry. Begin the ride from the main car park in the centre of the village, which has an information centre and public toilets.

DIRECTIONS

1. Leave the car park, with the Tourist Information Office behind you on the left, and at the exit turn right, signed 'Windermere'. In 100yds (91.5m), at the T-junction turn left, signed 'Windermere', and again after 100yds (91.5m) cross the beck and turn left, signed 'Wray'.

the lane between beech hedges and along the beck. Go straight on at the crossroads, climb the hill and after ½ mile (1km) turn left, signed 'Satterthwaite', and left again in a short distance. Continue past a picnic spot, to reach a T-junction opposite the post office at Force Mills.

5. Turn right here and enter Grizedale Forest Park, with the rapids of Force Mills on the left. After 1 mile (1.5km), enter Satterthwaite village, with the Eagle's Head pub on the left. Pass All Saints' Church on the right and the village green on the left and continue, to reach Grizedale Hall and Visitor Centre.

Continue for 3 miles (5km) past Grizedale Lodge Hotel to the top of the hill before descending to a T-junction. Turn left here to return to the centre of Hawkshead village and the start point of the ride.

Right: Grizedale Forest.
Below: Rhododendrons and azaleas flourish in the gardens of Graythwaite Hall

37

HELVELLYN
MOUNTAIN OFF A591, 4 MILES (6.5KM) W OF PATTERDALE

Overlooking Ullswater, the view from the top of Helvellyn (3,115ft/950m) is extensive, northwards towards Keswick and east to the Pennines, and thousands of fell walkers regularly make the journey to the summit. There are two approaches – from Wythburn on the south-eastern shores of Thirlmere reservoir which takes walkers up the steep south-western slopes, or from Grisedale or Glenridding to the east. A summit memorial quotes Wordsworth and Sir Walter Scott.

HOLKER HALL & GARDENS
OFF B5278, S OF NEWBY BRIDGE
TEL: 015395 58328

Dating from the 16th century, the new wing of the hall was rebuilt in 1871 after a disastrous fire. It has notable woodcarving and many fine pieces of furniture which mix happily with family photographs from the present day. Magnificent 25-acre (10-ha) award-winning gardens, both formal and woodland, are adjacent to the hall; here you will find a fantastic limestone cascade and other water features. The Lakeland Motor Museum, exhibitions, deer park and adventure playground are further attractions.
    Open Apr–Oct, most days.

HOLMBROOK
VILLAGE ON A595, 3 MILES (5KM) SE OF SEASCALE

A small village with St Paul's Church which contains a 9th-century cross of the Irish style and memorials to the Lutwidges, the family of Lewis Carroll.

HONISTER PASS
MOUNTAIN PASS ON B5289, W OF SEATOLLER

A steep stretch of road lying between Buttermere and Seatoller, with old quarry workings at the summit.

HUTTON-IN-THE-FOREST
ON B5305
TEL: 017684 84449

Hutton-in-the-Forest is a beautiful historic house set in magnificent woods which were once part of the medieval forest of Inglewood. The house consists of a 14th-century pele tower with additions from the 17th, 18th and 19th centuries. Inside is a fine collection of furniture, portraits, tapestries and china, a 17th-century gallery and cupid staircase. The lovely 1730s walled garden is a wonderful setting for the large collection of herbaceous plants. There are also 19th-century topiary terraces, a 17th-century dovecote and a woodland walk with impressive specimen trees.
    Open Apr–Sep, certain days.

Holker Hall, a charming house set amid formal and woodland gardens

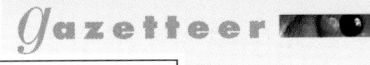

The crag at Hutton Roof is an area of Special Scientific Interest because of the limestone pavements and the flora which thrive here.

HUTTON ROOF
VILLAGE OFF A65, 3 MILES
(5KM) W OF KIRKBY LONSDALE

Today Kendal is famous for its Kendal Mint Cake, but it was once an important woollen textile centre, the industry having been founded by John Kemp, a Flemish weaver, in 1331. The town was also famous for its Kendal Bowmen, skilled archers clad in Kendal Green cloth, who fought against the Scots at the Battle of Flodden Field in 1513.

Catherine Parr, the last of Henry VIII's six wives, lived at Kendal Castle in the 16th century before she became Queen of England. Today the castle is a ruin, but Catherine Parr's Book of Devotions is housed in the town hall on Stricklandgate. A distinctive feature of the town's historic centre is the series of named or numbered yards, tucked away down alleyways and through arches, once the focus of local small industry.

The 13th-century parish church of Kendal, one of the largest in England, has five aisles and a peal of ten bells.

KENDAL
TOWN ON A6, 19 MILES
(30.5KM) N OF LANCASTER

The ground floor rooms of this splendid house in Kendal, reputedly designed in 1759 by John Carr of York, have been restored to their period decor, including the original carvings and fine panelling. The rooms make a perfect setting for the Gillow furniture and *objets d'art* displayed here, while the walls are hung with paintings by Romney, Gardner, Turner and Ruskin. The gallery has a fine collection of 18th- and 19th-century watercolours of the Lake District, and exceptionally good 20th-century British art, including works by Barbara Hepworth, Frink, Ben Nicholson, Sutherland, Piper and Hitchens.

Open daily, mid Feb–mid Dec.

Abbot Hall Art Gallery
KIRKLAND
TEL: 01539 722464

The life and history of the Lake District has a unique quality which is captured by the displays in this museum, housed in Abbot Hall's stable block. The working and social life of the area, its people and places are well illustrated by a variety of exhibits including period rooms, a Victorian Cumbrian street scene and a farming display. One of the rooms is devoted to the memory of Arthur Ransome, another to John Cunliffe's 'Postman Pat'.

Open daily, mid Feb–mid Dec.

Abbot Hall Museum of Lakeland Life & Industry
KIRKLAND
TEL: 01539 722464

The archaeology and natural history of the Lake District is explored in this popular museum which also features a world wildlife exhibition and a gallery devoted to Alfred Wainwright – the author who was honorary clerk to the museum.

Open daily, Mar–Dec.

Kendal Museum
STATION RD
TEL: 01539 721374

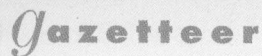

KENTDALE
VALLEY OFF STAVELEY, N OF A591

The valley begins at Staveley from where a minor road leads northwards, along the valley bottom and close to the River Kent, to the village of Kentmere. From Kentmere the head of the valley can be explored on foot.

KENTMERE
VILLAGE OFF A591, 4 MILES (6.5KM) N OF STAVELEY

The village is on the River Kent, which provided power for industry along its banks.

KESWICK
TOWN OFF A66, 16 MILES (25.5KM) W OF PENRITH

Keswick is the largest town within the Lake District National Park and the main tourist centre of northern Lakeland, situated on the shores of Derwent Water and separating the two distinctive areas of Skiddaw and Borrowdale. It developed as a focus for the mining industry in Elizabethan times, and German miners were brought in to help exploit the lead and copper deposits in the hills. Graphite was also mined in Borrowdale, resulting in the establishment of a pencil factory which has since operated with imported material. The Cumberland Pencil Museum has a realistic reconstruction of a section of a mine and uses exhibits, including the world's largest pencil, 7ft (2m) long, and a video to present the story of the industry.

Canon Rawnsley, one of the founders of the National Trust, was once vicar here.

Nearby Castlerigg Stone Circle, believed to have been erected 3,500 years ago, contains 38 boulders and measures 107ft (33m) across at its widest point.

Cars of the Stars Motor Museum
STANDISH STREET
TEL: 017687 73757

This unique collection features vehicles from the world of film and television including Del Boy's Robin Reliant in *Only Fools and Horses*, the Batmobile, a selection of cars used in the James Bond films and the Morris 8 Tourer driven by James Herriot in *All Creatures Great and Small*.

Open Feb half term–New Year, daily.

Keswick Museum & Art Gallery
FITZ PARK, STATION RD
TEL: 017687 73263

A mecca for writers, poets and artists, Keswick's attractions are well illustrated in this museum and gallery. Names such as Coleridge, Shelley, Wordsworth, Southey, Lamb and Walpole can be found among the exhibits which include letters, manuscripts and other relics from the time these literary luminaries spent in the Lake District. One of Ruskin's paintings is among the collections in the art gallery, and there is a fine scale model of the Lakes dating from 1834. The comprehensive geology collection is of national importance and contains magnificent mineral examples from the Caldbeck Fells. The natural history displays cover animal and bird life of the region,

The boat landings at Keswick on the shores of Derwent Water. The lake is a 20-minute walk from the town centre

including a golden eagle, and butterfly and moth cabinets. Fitz Park contains formal gardens and a children's adventure playground. There are monthly exhibitions by local artists and craft workers.

Open daily, Etr–Oct.

Both formal and woodland gardens are seen at Lingholm, which is at its most spectacular when the rhododendrons and azaleas are in bloom. The gardens include meconopsis, primulas, magnificent trees and shrubs, herbaceous borders and gentians. In spring, they are alive with daffodils, and the colours of autumn are breathtaking.

Open daily, Apr–Oct.

Lingholm Gardens
LINGHOLM, S OF A66, SIGNPOSTED FROM PORTINSCALE VILLAGE
TEL: 017687 72003

Undoubtedly a great place for children – there are four adventure playgrounds – but Mirehouse has its fair share of cultural interest, and a walk along the beautiful lake shore will take you past the place where Tennyson wrote much of *Morte d'Arthur*. Inside the 17th-century house much original furniture adorns the graceful rooms. Portraits and manuscripts of Francis Bacon, Carlyle and, of course, Tennyson are on display. Children are welcome with plenty of things to find and do including riding a large Victorian rocking horse. Outside, the flowers in the walled garden attract the bees and butterflies, and make this sheltered spot perfect for picnics. There is also a wildflower meadow and access to the 10th-century lakeside church. Mirehouse is also the venue for two concerts attached to Keswick Jazz Festival at the end of May, and bobbin lace demonstrations are held occasionally.

Open Apr–Oct. House: certain days; grounds: daily.

Mirehouse
3 MILES (5KM) N OF KESWICK ON A591
TEL: 017687 72287

A steep mountain pass (1,489ft/454m) named after the rock at the summit which looks like a church steeple. Near by is the Kirkstone Pass Inn, the third highest pub in the country.

KIRKSTONE PASS
MOUNTAIN PASS ON A592, 5 MILES (8KM) S OF PATTERDALE

THE
LAKE DISTRICT

The Lake District could be said to be where the National Parks movement began. In one of the first guidebooks to the area, William Wordsworth wrote that 'persons of pure taste' would 'deem the district a sort of national property, in which every man has a right and interest who has an eye to perceive and a heart to enjoy'. It was to be another 150 years before Wordsworth's dream became reality, and the Lake District became Britain's largest National Park. Today it is the same enchantingly beautiful accessible landscape of craggy mountains, shining lakes and reed-fringed tarns which first entranced Wordsworth and his fellow poets of the Romantic school.

It was in his best-selling Guide Through the District of the Lakes in the North of England, *first published in 1810, that William Wordsworth made the suggestion that it should become 'a sort of national property', a statement which is now generally regarded as the genesis of the National Park movement. It was Wordsworth, too, who started the more general appreciation of the Lake District as a place to visit with his guide which, 180 years later, is still in print. He broke the mould of previous guidebooks which, with one or two notable exceptions, had regarded this craggy, mountainous area with something approaching mortal terror. It should be remembered that before Wordsworth and his fellow Romantics began to find beauty and inspiration in rugged, natural scenery like that of the Lakes, such places were universally regarded as blots, rather than beauty spots, on the landscape.*

The earliest travellers to the Lakes were filled with fear and trepidation as they cautiously made their way, using guides, into these 'horrid' and 'frightful' places. One of the first was the journalist Daniel Defoe,

Autumn in the Lakes, Ullswater near Glenridding

Coniston, from the eastern shore of Coniston Water

who wrote in his Tour Through the Whole Island of Great Britain *(1724) that Westmorland was 'a country eminent only for being the wildest, most barren and frightful of any that I have passed over in England, or even in Wales itself...' He saw nothing but 'an inhospitable terror' in the Lakeland hills and, reflecting the feelings of his day, he added that it was 'of no advantage to represent horror as the character of a country...'*

Defoe was not alone in expressing his feeling in this way. Dr John Brown, describing the vale and lake of Keswick in 1769, saw only 'rocks and cliffs of stupendous heights, hanging broken over the lake in horrible grandeur'. Thomas Gray, author of the famous Elegy Written in a Country Churchyard, *also dared go no further into the jaws of Borrowdale, explaining to his readers that 'all farther access is here barr'd to prying Mortals'. William Gilpin described the ascent of Dunmail Raise from Grasmere thus: 'The whole view is entirely of the*

horrid kind... Of all the scenes I ever saw, this was the most adapted to the perpetration of some dreadful deed.' Yet more and more *'persons of pure taste'* were finding pleasure in picturesque landscapes, encouraged by artists like J M W Turner, John Constable and Thomas Gainsborough who, quite literally, were putting the Lakes in the picture. As the appreciation of landscape increased, a movement – led by Wordsworth and the school of writers attracted to the Lakes by his poetry – to preserve it all began.

Wordsworth was also the first of the upper-class preservationists who really wanted to keep the scenery just for themselves. They feared the results of allowing, as he put it, *'artisans, labourers and the humbler class of shopkeeper'* into the area. When an extension of the main railway line to Kendal and Windermere was proposed, he fumed in a famous sonnet:

> *Is then no nook of English ground*
> > *secure*
> *From rash assault?*

This elitist attitude was to become a common one among Wordsworth's fellow Romantics. Later John Ruskin, who lived for the last years of his life at Brantwood beside Coniston Water, complained of *'the certainty of the deterioration of the moral character in the inhabitants of every district penetrated by a railway'*. He objected to the railway engineers *'making a steam merry-go-round of the lake country'*, and as for the resultant incoming tourists, Ruskin declared imperiously: *'I don't want them to see Helvellyn while they are drunk'*. Despite these apparent double standards, it was from among this social class that the first moves to protect the Lake District came. Canon Hardwicke Rawnsley, incumbent at Crosthwaite near Keswick, became one of the founding fathers of the National Trust. Now the biggest single private landowner in the 885 square mile (2,292sq km) National Park, the Trust owns about a third of the area and manages

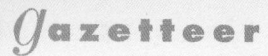

it in a way which would no doubt delight those early pioneer preservationists.

People such as Rawnsley were also great walkers, and this tradition has been perpetuated to this day by the works of the late Alfred Wainwright (among others), former borough treasurer at Kendal, whose immaculately hand-crafted but sadly unrevised Pictorial Guides to the Lakeland Fells now rival Wordsworth's guide in sales. Thomas de Quincy, the opium-smoking poet who was a close friend of the Wordsworths and took over the lease of Dove Cottage at Grasmere when William and his devoted sister, Dorothy, moved out to Rydal Mount, estimated that William's legs, which he describes as 'certainly not ornamental', covered between 175,000 (280,000) and 180,000 miles (288,000km) in his lifetime.

Samuel Taylor Coleridge, another of the Lakes School, is credited with undertaking one of the first recorded rock climbs in the area when he successfully negotiated a descent via Broad Stand after climbing Scafell Pike, at 3,206ft (977m) the highest point in England, while on a 100-mile (160-km) walking tour in 1802.

It was to be another 84 years before the sport of rock climbing was launched in the Lake District by Walter Haskett Smith's solo ascent of Napes Needle, the sharply pointed pinnacle on the side of 2,949-ft (899-m) high Great Gable. In his graphic account of that pioneering climb, Smith described himself as 'feeling as small as a mouse climbing a milestone'.

Rock climbing, especially in Borrowdale and Wasdale, still attracts large numbers of climbers to the Lakes, but the majority of the estimated 20 million annual visitors to this famous British National Park, set up in 1951, follow in Wordsworth's and Wainwright's steps and wander the fells on foot. With free and open access to most of

Rowing boats moored in the reeds at Grasmere

the hills, and a well-maintained and signposted network of 1,500 miles (2,400km) of public rights of way in the valleys, there is a lifetime of walking within the boundaries of the Park. However, pressure on the most popular paths inevitably brings problems in its wake, and major restoration work has had to be undertaken by both the National Park authority and the National Trust to combat the effects of human erosion. Staircases of natural rock have had to be installed on popular summits such as Helm Crag, near the Wordsworths' home at Grasmere, perhaps realising some of the fears of William Wordsworth and John Ruskin.

Other honeypots to be avoided on busy summer weekends are Windermere, where a 10-mph (16-kph) speed limit was imposed on England's biggest lake to curb water-skiers and powerboats; Tarn Hows, the quaint village set in a pretty though man-made, landscape near the village of Hawkshead where William Wordsworth went to school and the Langdale valley, where the twin-topped Langdale Pikes provide an irresistible lure for the hill walker.

Derwent Water from Friar's Crag viewpoint

Wordsworth, a keen observer of the landscape, was the first to compare the topography of the Lake District to the radiating spokes of a wheel, and the mountains and dales, most containing lakes or tarns, do seem to spread out from a central point around about Dunmail Raise, the highest point on the A591 between Grasmere and Keswick. The Lake District's most distinguished modern poet, Norman Nicholson, has more accurately compared the shape with that of a lemon-squeezer because the dales are gouged out of a dome and slope outwards to a lower rim.

Three major types of rock are encountered in the Lake District. The Silurian slates create the softer, well-wooded landscapes found around Windermere and Coniston Water in the south, while the Borrowdale volcanics, dating from the Ordovician period, give the rugged, craggy features of Borrowdale, Langdale, Helvellyn and Wasdale in the central part of the district. The older Skiddaw slates have created the steep but usually smooth shapes of the northern fells which include Skiddaw, Blencathra and Grisedale Pike, and which echo the Howgill Fells across the Lune Gorge. Surrounding the Park is a border of carboniferous limestone.

The most important agent which shaped the Lake District we see today was the enormous crushing, grinding, chiselling power of Ice Age glaciers. Centred on the middle of the district for several thousand years, they created the 'radiating wheel' formation first noted by Wordsworth, and scooped out the U-shaped dales within which most of the lakes now lie. Everywhere you look you can see signs of the passing glaciers which did not disappear until about 10,000 years ago – relatively recently in the vast geological timescale. The strange, rounded, grassy hillocks – drumlins – which can be seen alongside the A591 at Dunmail Raise were left by the retreating glaciers, and from the summit of the pass, between the summits of Seat Sandal and Steel Fell, the classic U-shape of glaciated valleys is very evident.

Up in the hills, usually on the north or north-eastern slopes of the mountains, corries (locally known as coves) have been scooped out by snow and glacial action, often leaving a jewel-like tarn at their heart. Good examples can be seen at Red Tarn on Helvellyn, Scales Tarn on Blencathra, Levers Water on Coniston Old Man, and Blea Water, the deepest of all, on High Street above the flooded vale of Haweswater.

The pedant will tell you that, in fact, there is only one lake in the Lake District because Bassenthwaite Lake in the north-west of the National

Park is the only one actually called a lake. All the rest take the older names of mere, or water, and the smaller lakes, the tarns, take their name from the Old Norse word, tjorn. Many other Norse names crop up on the Lake District map, such as thwaite, meaning a clearing for pasture; fell, meaning a mountain; and seat, meaning a hill pasture used in the summer. The abundance of these ancient names shows the origins of the early farmers and shepherds of these hills, although they were not the first to walk the fells by any means.

One of the most atmospheric places in the Lake District is the Neolithic stone circle at Castlerigg, a few miles outside Keswick. Here, on an elevated pasture backed by the smooth slopes of Blencathra and Skiddaw to the north and the Helvellyn range to the south, stands the most impressive prehistoric monument in the National Park. Described by John Keats on a visit in 1818 as 'A dismal cirque of Druid stones upon a forlorn moor', Castlerigg is thought to have been some kind of religious centre, but no-one can be sure. Evidence of prehistoric industrial activity was found in 1947 on the steep scree slopes below Pike of Stickle, one of the Langdale Pikes. Here the site of a stone axe factory was identified. These elegant tools were literally at the cutting edge of Stone Age technology and the craftsmen who shaped them certainly knew their geology for they chose the fine-grained, hardened tuff found among the Borrowdale volcanics for their raw material. The axes, which were later exported all over Britain, were finally shaped and finished at sites on the coast. Since the Langdale discovery several other axe factories have been identified, one close to the summit of Scafell Pike – surely the highest industrial site in Britain. The Romans also stamped their imperial mark on the Lake District and when motorists embark on one of the most exciting car drives in Britain, across the Wrynose and Hardknott Passes between Ambleside and Ravenglass, they are following in the footsteps of the Roman legions who built forts at either end of the route. Just below the head of the pass, on a green 800-ft (243-m) spur under Border End, are the

well-preserved remains of the Roman fort of Mediobogdum, one of the most remote and impressive Roman sites in Britain.

However, it was Viking raiders from the north who first tamed the wild Lake District landscape, and nowhere gives a better impression of a Norse settlement than the tiny hamlet of Watendlath, high above the deep, wooded vale of Borrowdale, just south of Derwent Water. The name is thought to mean 'the barn at the end of the lake', and it is still a pretty accurate description of the spot today. A collection of grey-stoned farm buildings cluster round the head of a reed-fringed tarn at the end of a narrow, dead-end road which winds up past the popular viewpoint of Ashness Bridge, above Derwent Water. Hills with Norse names such as High Seat, Great Crag and Rough Knott frown down on the secret valley which looks as if it has been transported from Arctic Norway. Beautiful little rowan-fringed Dock Tarn, across the fells to the south of Watendlath, is decorated by the white flowers of waterlilies. The name comes from the Old Norse and means 'the tarn of the waterlilies'.

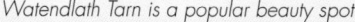

Watendlath Tarn is a popular beauty spot

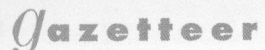
LAKESIDE & HAVERTHWAITE RAILWAY

In the valley of the River Leven, S of lake Windermere

Tel: *015395 31594*

Steaming out of Haverthwaite Station

It is a cruel irony that the Lakeland poets, and in particular Wordsworth, created a fascination for the romantic beauty of the district and then felt compelled to turn their pens to resisting the means whereby large numbers could enjoy it. However, it was the other railway to reach the shore of Windermere, the still open Kendal & Windermere, that was the subject of Wordsworth's vitriolic poem. By the time the Furness Railway reached Lakeside in 1869, Wordsworth had been dead for 19 years.

The headquarters of the 3½-mile (5.5-km) Lakeside & Haverthwaite Railway is at the latter station, curiously positioned between two unlined tunnels, like the bizarrely sited stations beside the Ligurian Sea between Genoa and La Spezia. The original idea was to connect with

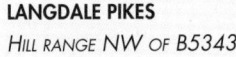

the main railway line further south at Plympton, but a road-widening scheme put paid to it. The tank locomotives that operate the line have a stiff climb out of Haverthwaite, running parallel with a line that served Backbarrow Ironworks until it closed in 1967. The finest views are over the Leven Valley to the east of the line, with the river frequently in sight. A large factory producing ultramarine (Reckitt's Blue) is passed on the right, and – more picturesquely – a waterfall and adjacent mill can be seen before the small halt at Newby Bridge is reached. It was while staying at the Newby Bridge Hotel in 1931 that Arthur Ransome wrote *Swallows and Amazons*. The halt, used during World War II to bring prisoners to the Grizedale Hall prisoner-of-war camp, is the start of a number of fine walks. But visitors should not miss the section of the line from here to Lakeside for it is the most scenic part, passing through oakwoods and skirting the southern end of lake Windermere.

The station buildings provided by the Furness Railway for its train and steamer services at Lakeside were so splendid that some shareholders complained of extravagance. Sadly they were almost entirely demolished before the Lakeside & Haverthwaite took over. However, steamers still connect with trains for a 3½-hour cruise of the lake, which can be prolonged by visiting the Windermere Steam Boat Museum (see page 91). Amongst the elegant vessels in its collection is the steam yacht *Esperance*, which Arthur Ransome immortalised as the houseboat in *Swallows and Amazons*.

Train service: end Mar–beginning Apr & May–Oct daily.

LANGDALE PIKES
HILL RANGE NW OF B5343

A spectacular range of high peaks. Great Langdale Valley is a sweeping glaciated valley with steep sides and a wide, flat bottom. There is a National Trust campsite in Great Langdale and car park beneath Stickle Ghyll. Stickle Ghyll Force drops 128ft (38m) on to boulders. Old Dungeon Ghyll Hotel was given to the National Trust by historian G M Trevelyan.

LEVENS HALL

*5 MILES (8KM) S OF KENDAL
ON A6*

TEL: 01539 560321

Standing at the head of the estuary of the River Kent, close to Kendal, are the amazing gardens of Levens Hall. To most people, Levens is known for its topiary, and the formal layout has a strong flavour of the 17th century. But the garden's links with the adjoining park, now unhappily separated by the A6, show the beginnings of the naturalised gardening movement of the beginning of the 18th century which was to have such a profound influence on the appearance of English gardens and, indeed, of our countryside.

There has been a fortified pele tower on the site of Levens since the 12th century, but the grim medieval building was later turned into a gentleman's residence, and in 1690 Colonel James Grahme began to make it into the finest house in Cumbria, engaging a Monsieur Guillaume Beaumont, who had trained under Le Nôtre at Versailles and worked for King James II at Hampton Court, to lay out the gardens. Today, still immaculately maintained by the owner, Mr C H Bagot, the cones, spirals, pyramids and other geometric shapes in clipped yew and dark green and golden box are still there to be seen, as well as the topiary figures with their own names, such as 'The Judge's Wig' and 'Queen Elizabeth and her Maids of Honour'.

Beneath the great topiary specimens; many of them 20ft (6m) high, are narrow paths and box-edged beds planted with a riot of seasonal colour – primroses, forget-me-nots, wallflowers, begonias, antirrhinums and geraniums amongst them. Behind the topiary garden a border runs along the walls to the old orchard, and the previous owner, Mr Robin Bagot, planted this with a variety of climbers and shrubs, including clematis, philadelphus, ceanothus and old fruit trees. Beyond the great battlement of the yew hedge is the old orchard, which has flower borders leading to the tall beech hedges, also planted by Beaumont. In summer, soft colours, particularly blue, line the grassy path, making this an enchanting place. Another grass walk lined with borders leads from the circular beech enclosure to one of the earliest ha-has in the country. A steam collection adds further interest.

When you cross the A6 you enter the only surviving Elizabethan deer park in the Kendal area. An avenue of splendid oaks planted in

the 18th century complements the winding river valley, and you might see the rare Bagot goats and fallow deer. Levens Hall is a magical place, redolent of a period when so many of our modern gardening practices were in their infancy.

Open Apr–Sep, most days.

A popular beauty spot. Small cascades splash through rocks in the woods to the 40-ft (12-m) waterfall, which is especially impressive after heavy rain.

The parterre garden at Levens Hall

LODORE FALLS
WATERFALL NEAR S END OF DERWENT WATER

LORTON, LOW AND HIGH
VILLAGES ON B5292, 4 MILES
(6.5KM) SE OF COCKERMOUTH

The villages have retained their traditional character and most of the houses are 150 to 300 years old. Both George Fox, the founder of the Quaker movement, and John Wesley, the Methodist, have preached here. There is a 1,000-year-old yew tree which was immortalised in Wordsworth's poem 'Yew Trees'.

LOWESWATER
LAKE AND HAMLET W OF
B5289, 6 MILES (9.5KM)
S OF COCKERMOUTH

The lake lies in the Buttermere Valley and is National Trust owned. The scattered hamlet of Loweswater looks over Crummock Water to Buttermere; which is said to be one of the region's loveliest views.
(See also Cycle ride: The Cockermouth Circuit, page 12.)

LOWTHER
HAMLET OFF A6, 4 MILES
(6.5KM) S OF PENRITH

Home of the Lowther family from 1283. They lived originally at Lowther Hall, much of which was burnt down in 1720, until Lowther Castle was built in the early 19th century. Today Lowther Castle is an impressive, but empty, shell. Lowther village was designed in the 1780s by the Adam brothers. 'Hughie' Lowther, 5th Earl of Lonsdale, instituted the Lonsdale Belt, was first president of the Automobile Association. The 150-acre (61-ha) Lowther Leisure Park has open-air and wet-weather attractions, along with peaceful scenic walks.
(See also Cycle ride: Penrith and Northern Lakeland, page 62.)

MARYPORT
TOWN ON A596, 6 MILES
(10KM) NE OF WORKINGTON

The harbour at the mouth of the River Ellen was a considerable ship-building centre up to the end of the 19th century.

Maritime Museum
1 SENHOUSE STREET
TEL: 01900 813738

The museum houses a wealth of objects, models and paintings that illustrate Maryport's maritime traditions. Mutineer Fletcher Christian and the ship-owner Thomas Henry Ismay, founder of the great White Star Line, the company which built the *Titanic*, are both featured here.
Open all year; restricted winter opening.

MILLOM
TOWN ON A5098, 5 MILES
(8KM) SW OF BROUGHTON-IN-FURNESS

A small industrial town on the coast with splendid surrounding beaches. In 1868 a rich seam of haematite was discovered at the tip of the peninsula at Hodbarrow, and Millom was built to work the mine. Working of the seam stopped 100 years later.

Millom Folk Museum
ST GEORGE'S ROAD
TEL: 01229 772555

All the exhibits in this museum illustrate local life, and they are presented in an informative and captivating way with reconstructed room sets of a miner's cottage; a blacksmith's forge, complete with tools; a corner shop; and a full-scale model of a drift of the Hodbarrow Iron Ore Mine. There is also a tribute to the late Dr Norman C Nicholson, poet and author of *A Man of Millom*.
Open Etr wk, May Day wknd and Spring—mid Sep, most days.

Diverse attractions are offered at this castle, the seat of the Pennington family since the 13th century. Inside is a fine collection of 16th- and 17th-century furnishings, embroideries and portraits, whilst the grounds have a nature trail, a children's play area, and a profusion of rhododendrons, camellias, magnolias and azaleas. There is also an extensive collection of owls, from the pygmy owl to the gigantic eagle owl, as this is the headquarters of the World Owl Trust. Closed circuit television on some nests allows an intimate look, and there are continuous owl videos throughout the day in the Old Diary Theatre. Daily 'Meet the Birds' sessions take place from April until October when talks are given on the work of the Owl Centre and, weather permitting, the birds fly.

Open: Castle, end Mar–Oct most afternoons; Garden & Owl Centre: all year, daily.

(See also Muncaster Walk, page 58.)

MUNCASTER CASTLE, GARDENS & OWL CENTRE
1 MILE (1.5KM) E OF RAVENGLASS ON A595
TEL: 01229 717614 & 717393 (OWL CENTRE)

There has been a mill on this site since the 15th century, and flour and oatmeal are still ground on the premises. The water is brought three-quarters of a mile from the River Mite to the 13-ft (4-m) overshot water wheel, and all the milling equipment is water driven. This old manorial mill is served by the Ravenglass and Eskdale Railway.

Open Apr–Oct, daily.

(See also Muncaster Walk, page 58.)

MUNCASTER WATER MILL
1 MILE (1.5KM) NW OF RAVENGLASS ON A595
TEL: 01229 717232

This village is in a pretty setting in the northern fells, with a stream, pub, hotel and old church.

MUNGRISDALE
HAMLET OFF A66, 8 MILES (13KM) NE OF KESWICK

Some of the magnificent azaleas in the gardens of Muncaster Castle

*A*t the head of Eskdale lie the highest mountains in Lakeland, and at its foot are the dunes and estuary of Ravenglass. This walk incorporates a trip on a miniature railway, a water mill, a castle and a Roman ruin.

Grid ref: SD085964

INFORMATION

After the train ride, the walk is about 3 miles (5km) long. Some steep sections, but not difficult underfoot. Several gates and a stile. Short sections of road walking, one with a pavement, the other on a quiet private road. Refreshment facilities in Ravenglass, including the Ratty Arms next to the railway station. There is a café at Muncaster Castle.

START

Ravenglass is just off the A595 about 5 miles (8km) south of Gosforth. Park at the Ravenglass and Eskdale Railway and catch a train. There is an hourly service up the valley (for times and charges, tel: 01229 717171). Alight at the first stop, Muncaster Mill, and the walk starts here.

DIRECTIONS

From Muncaster Mill station go through the mill yard and up the track, past the old wheel machinery and chicken sheds, then turn right along a bridleway, signposted 'Castle' and 'Ravenglass'. Walk along the bridleway for about 20yds (18m). Two paths lead off to the left. Take the first of these, signposted 'Castle'. Walk up the rather steep path, through woodland, until this levels off and meets a track. Go straight on following a dip between wooded ridges for

about ½ mile (1km). At the end of the woodland, go through a gate and turn left.

At the road (A595) go through a gate and straight on, downhill along the pavement, then cross the road with care and go through the gates of Muncaster Castle.

Walk down the drive signposted 'Muncaster Church' and 'Footpath to Ravenglass', past the stables, garden centre and café. At the end of the drive, go straight across the lawns, with waterfowl pens to your right, to meet another drive. Cross this and follow a track uphill, signposted 'Ravenglass via Newtown'. At the end of this wooded track, go over the stile and out on to the open hill top.

The route is signposted but the path is not obvious; follow the direction indicated by the signpost, to the right of the hill crest. At isolated gate posts,

WHAT TO LOOK OUT FOR

The woods of Muncaster Castle contain some very exotic trees. The castle itself is only a century old, built on to fragments of a 14th-century tower house.
Walls Castle has a much better pedigree but is no more than a ruin. In fact it began as a Roman bathhouse, associated with the fort of Glannaventa which lies buried on the other side of the track.
From the top of the hill there are fine views of Ravenglass Dunes (a nature reserve) and the Esk estuary. In the distance to the north is Sellafield Nuclear Power Station.

continue ahead to the plantation with the rooftops of Newtown just beyond. Cross the stile and walk downhill through the plantation to go through a gate and turn along a broad track, passing a house on the left. On reaching a metalled private road, turn right past Roman bathhouse ruins on the right, then continue to the end of the road, passing Walls Caravan Park. Just after the gates is a footpath on the left which leads to Ravenglass station the start point of the walk.

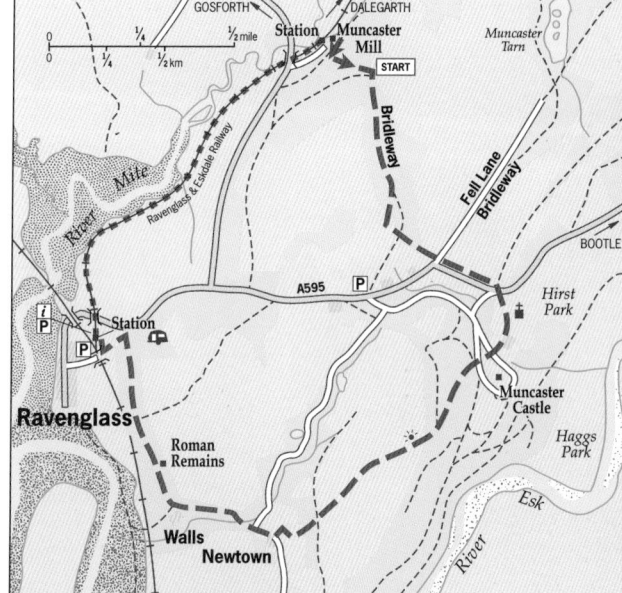

Muncaster Mill is the first stop for the train

The Ravenglass & Eskdale Railway

The Eskdale narrow-gauge railway, opened in 1875 to carry iron ore from Boot to Ravenglass, is now a popular tourist attraction. (See also page 68.)

Muncaster Castle and Owl Centre

Diverse attractions are offered at this castle, seat of the Pennington family since the 13th century. (See also page 57.)

Muncaster Mill

There has been a mill on this site since the late 15th century, and flour and oatmeal are still ground on the premises using water power from the 13-ft (4-m) waterwheel. (See also page 57.)

NEAR SAWREY AND FAR SAWREY

VILLAGES OFF A592, 3 MILES (5KM) SW OF BOWNESS-ON-WINDERMERE

Both villages are situated between lake Windermere and Esthwaite Water. Near Sawrey is furthest from the ferry from Bowness-on-Windermere. Beatrix Potter first came to Near Sawrey in 1896 when her parents rented a house in the village called Lakeland. Later, the author bought Hill Top with the royalties from *The Tale of Peter Rabbit* (1900).

Hill Top

TEL: 015394 36269

Beatrix Potter wrote many of her Peter Rabbit books in this little 17th-century house which contains her furniture and china. The house and the adjacent inn, the Tower Bank Arms, which will be familiar to readers of *The Tale of Jemima Puddleduck* (1908), are both in the care of the National Trust. It is best to avoid the peak holiday times, particularly mornings in the school holidays, as Hill Top is a very small house and only a limited number of visitors can be admitted at one time.

Open Apr–Nov, most days.

gazetteer

A village on the River Kent which got its name from the five-arched stone bridge built in 1651 to replace the existing timber structure.

At the southern tip of Ullswater, in the shadow of Helvellyn, Patterdale is a popular little tourist village. St Patrick's Church, built in 1853, has notable tapestries by Ann Macbeth, who lived in the village from 1921 until her death in 1948, aged 73. Famous sheepdog trials called the Patterdale Dog Day are held on the Late Summer Bank Holiday. Here visitors can marvel at the ability of man and dog to work together and control a group of sheep. Gummer's How, to the north, is an excellent viewpoint.

NEWBY BRIDGE
VILLAGE OFF A590, 8 MILES (13KM) NE OF ULVERSTON

PATTERDALE
VILLAGE ON A592, S OF ULLSWATER

Main picture: Hill Top at Near Sawrey was the home of Beatrix Potter

Left: St Patrick's Church, Patterdale

*T*his route explores the north-eastern fringes of the Lake District with its diverse scenery, offering good views of the area's mountains and lakes and an insight into rural Cumbrian life. The area is rich in history – raided and settled by the Romans, Saxons, Normans, Scandinavians and Scots – and castles and fortified farmhouses are evidence of the turbulent past. The middle section is hilly but the effort is rewarded by fine views.

INFORMATION

Total Distance
25 miles (40km)

Difficulty
Challenging

OS Maps
Landranger 1:50,000 sheet 90
(West Cumbria)

Tourist Information
Penrith, tel: 01768 867466;
Pooley Bridge, tel: 017684
86530

Cycle Shops/Hire
Arragon Cycle Centre, Penrith,
tel: 01768 890344; Harpers,

At Pooley Bridge on Ullswater

Penrith, tel: 01768 864475;
Ullswater Caravan, Camping and
Marine Park, Watermillock, tel:
017684 86666; Tindals,
Gelridding/Pooley Bridge, tel:
017684 82393; The Sun Hotel,
Pooley Bridge, tel: 017684
86205

Nearest Railway Station
Penrith

Refreshments

Numerous pubs and cafés along the route, plus tea rooms and plenty of picnic spots, particularly at Wetheriggs Pottery, Lowther Park and Pooley Bridge.

START

Penrith lies by the M6 at junction 40. Park in the Southend Road pay-and-display car park at the south end of the town.

DIRECTIONS

1. Leave the car park going east, turn left into Southend Road then right into Crown Square. At the T-junction turn right into King Street then second left into Roper Street which becomes Carleton Road. Continue to the junction, turn right on to the A686, then immediately left and right again passing the Cross Keys pub on your left (ignore the 'no through road' sign). Follow the road downhill. At the end pass through the gate and follow a track under the A6. Turn left immediately to reach the road, then right, crossing the River Eamont with Brougham Castle on your right.

2. Continue with views of Cross Fell and the Pennines to the left,

The River Eamont flows past Brougham Castle

shortly cross the B6262 and continue for 3 miles (2km) to reach a T-junction at Clifton Dykes. Turn left, signed 'Wetheriggs Pottery', and continue for ½ mile (1km) to Wetheriggs Country Pottery.

3. Continue for 650yds (600m) then turn right signed 'Melkinthorpe'. Follow this road, passing under the railway to reach the A6. Turn left then second right and follow signs for

Lowther. Just past Lowther village is the Lakeland Bird of Prey Centre.

4. Continue through Newtown; at the end of the line of houses, where the road bears right, continue straight on following the sign for Askham and Ullswater. At the T-junction by the knobbly oak tree turn left, cross over the cattle grid, pass through the park with Lowther Castle on your left and carefully descend a steep hill to eventually cross the river and pass St Peter's Church and climb into Askham.

5. At the T-junction at the top of the green, turn right, signed 'Ullswater', passing the village

Barton Church at Pooley Bridge is an impressive sight

shop and the Queen's Head. Continue for 550yds (500m) before turning left, signed 'Celleron', to climb with views of High Street on the left and the Pennines on the right. Continue ahead to the next T-junction (B5320) and turn left. Passing Barton Hall on the right, in 1½ miles (2.5km) enter Pooley Bridge. (From here you may shorten the route by 5 miles/8km if you return to Penrith by retracing the route along the B5320, continuing for 5 miles/8km through Sockbridge, Tirril, and Yanwath to the junction with the A6. Turn left and proceed with care over Eamont Bridge and back into Penrith.)

6. Go over the bridge and continue on the B5320, passing the ferry jetty on your left. Soon

turn right on to the A592, signed 'Penrith', and after 1 mile (1.5km) turn left signed 'Dacre'. Follow the lane, eventually descending to cross the beck, and shortly arrive in Dacre. Leave Dacre by the narrow lane on the left as you entered the village, signed 'Sparket and Thackthwaite'. After 1½ miles (2.5km), at a crossroads turn right, signed 'Penruddock'. Continue past Hutton John Hall, enjoying the views of the Lakeland mountains as you climb, eventually crossing the A66 (with care), to join the flat lanes leading to Greystoke.

7. Leave the village following the road signed 'Johnby and Blencow', and shortly bear right, signed 'Blencow and Carlisle'. Pass Blencow Hall (a fortified farmhouse) and continue through

Cycle ride

ittle Blencow. After ½ mile (1km) urn right, signed 'Laithes'. Follow his road, with views of Cross Fell, hrough Laithes (Cattellen Hall on he right) and Newton Reigny to eturn to Penrith. Follow signs for he town centre and return to the car park and the start of the ride.

PLACES OF INTEREST

Penrith
Gateway to the Northern Lakes, his former capital of Cumbria and how the hub of the Eden Valley is a busy market town with much to offer the visitor.
(See also page 66.)

Brougham Castle
On the banks of the River Eamont ie the ruins of one of the region's strongest castles, built in the 13th

century and restored in the 17th by Lady Anne Clifford.
(See also page 8.)

Wetheriggs Country Pottery
A working pottery with a museum and a nature trail.
(See also page 67.)

Lowther
The Lakeland Birds of Prey Centre is situated in the grounds of Lowther Castle. There are daily

Historic Gloucester Arms in the busy market town of Penrith

flying demonstrations between March and October.
(See also page 56.)

Pooley Bridge
At the northern end of Ullswater, Pooley Bridge offers magnificent views of the mountains. There are steamer trips during the summer.
(See also page 67.)

WHAT TO LOOK OUT FOR

There are many opportunities to glimpse a wide variety of wild life, particularly red squirrel, roe deer, buzzard, kestrel and sparrow hawks. Look too for fortified farmhouses (halls) at Little Blencow, Laithes, Hutton John and Yanwath, and castles at Penrith, Brougham, Lowther and Dacre.

PENRITH

*TOWN OFF M6, 18 MILES
(29KM) SE OF CARLISLE*

In the 9th and 10th centuries Penrith was the capital of Cumbria and defended the surrounding country from marauding Scots. The castle was built around 1399 and enlarged for the Duke of Gloucester (later Richard III) when he was Warden of the Western Marches and responsible for keeping the peace along the border with Scotland.

Today Penrith is a busy market town with a mixture of narrow streets and wide open spaces, such as Great Dockray, a large market place. St Andrew's Church dates from Norman times but the most recent part, the nave, was rebuilt between 1719 and 1772. Of particular interest are the three-sided gallery and the brass candelabra suspended from the roof, a gift from the Duke of Cumberland in 1745 – a reward for the town's loyalty during the Jacobite Rising.

The town hall, by Robert Adam (1791), was originally two houses, one of which was known as the Wordsworth House as it was the home of the poet's cousin, Captain John Wordsworth.

(See also Cycle ride: Penrith and Northern Lakeland, page 62.)

Penrith Castle has been in ruins since 1550, but remains an impressive monument

gazetteer

Wetheriggs Country Pottery has been working since 1855 and is steeped in rich traditions and set in a nature conservation site. See top crafts workers hand-throwing pots and take an educational tour around the surviving steam-powered pottery. Visitors have the opportunity to hand-throw their own pot.

Open Etr–Sep daily, telephone for winter opening.

Wetheriggs Country Pottery
*CLIFTON DYKES, 4 MILES
(6.5KM) S, OFF A6*
TEL: 01768 892733

A pretty village where small boats are moored, at the northern end of Ullswater. An attractive 16th-century bridge across the River Eamont leads to the village square.

(See also Cycle ride: Penrith and Northern Lakeland, page 62.)

POOLEY BRIDGE
*VILLAGE ON B5320, AT NE
END OF ULLSWATER*

The village was a Roman naval base, and a centre for pearl-fishing and smuggling until the harbour silted up. Today it comprises a short street of houses with a slipway down to the beach.

(See also Muncaster Walk, page 58.)

RAVENGLASS
*VILLAGE ON A595, 4 MILES
(6.5KM) SE OF SEASCALE*

RAVENGLASS & ESKDALE RAILWAY

AT RAVENGLASS, VILLAGE ON A595 4 MILES (6.5KM) SE OF SEASCALE

TEL: 01229 717171

It would be hard to quibble with the claim of the Ravenglass & Eskdale Railway that no other miniature railway in Britain passes through such magnificent scenery. Nor is that laurel likely to be taken away, since approval would never be given for such a railway today, passing as it does through the Lake District National Park for much of its length of almost 7 miles (11km). Its origins go back to 1875 when a line was opened from the old Roman port of Ravenglass to haematite mines in Eskdale. Both mines and railway were soon in financial difficulties, but the latter soldiered on, carrying both freight and passengers along its length until 1913.

That would have been the end of the 'Ratty', as it has long been known locally, had it not been for the Northampton model engineer and architect W J Bassett-Lowke. He leased the line, reduced the gauge from 3ft to 15in and re-opened it to tourists and later to stone traffic. Despite some serious ups and downs since then, its future has been secured because enough people delighted in its character, which in large measures stems from the beauty of Eskdale. The famous writer of Lake District walking books, Alfred Wainwright, regarded Eskdale as 'the finest of all valleys for those whose special joy is to travel on foot, and a paradise for artists'.

Most people begin their journey at the Ravenglass end, which can be reached by train from either Carlisle or from Carnforth and Barrow-in-Furness; both lines hug the coast and are highly recommended. The Ravenglass & Eskdale has almost taken over the main line station at Ravenglass – the main building is a pub, the Ratty Arms, the waiting room on the opposite platform is a well-presented museum about the railway's history, and the goods shed has been converted into workshops.

Trains for the 40-minute journey to Dalegarth/Eskdale leave from the adjacent three-platform station. You pass the signal box – which pioneered radio signalling in Britain – more workshops, the engine shed and the new carriage shed as the train leaves Ravenglass and heads for the first halt at Muncaster Mill (see page 57). In the distance can be seen another 'first' – the world's first atomic power station at Calder Hall, now Sellafield. The River Mite accompanies the train on its approach to Muncaster Mill and farm. Flour has been ground on this site since at least 1455, though today's recently renovated structure dates from about 1700. Organic flour is now ground daily and sold to visitors.

Throughout the journey an unfolding series of panoramas of the Lakeland mountains opens up – Steeple, Pillar, Great Gable, Scafell and Scafell Pike. For the latter part of the journey Harter Fell is the dominant peak, seen in the distance to the right. The line itself passes

through a mix of open pasture fringed with drystone walls and woods of birch and conifers. Bracken, gorse and heather cover some of the slopes, making this a line to beckon visitors in all seasons to experience the variety of colours.

Journey's end at Dalegarth is an opportunity to examine the locomotive as it moves on to the turntable or takes water for the return. The railway's six steam locomotives date from 1900 to 1976 and have to be capable of hauling up to 25-ton trains on the steep gradients. The oldest, *Bonnie Dundee*, was built for Dundee's gasworks and has had to be regauged, but the veteran is *Synolda*. This octogenarian from Bassett-Lowke's works dates from 1912 and was the first 15in-gauge Ravenglass & Eskdale locomotive. It is used only on special occasions, lacking the power and relative youth of the other original engines.

The railway is unusual in running a service on almost every day of the year, but during winter weekdays it starts from Eskdale, reflecting the importance of any public transport to the remote valley community. To operate these services the Ravenglass & Eskdale Railway has a number of diesel locomotives.

Trains operate all year, Mar–Nov & between Xmas & New Year daily; wknds only Dec–Feb. Limited service Jan & Feb except during school hols.

The Ravenglass & Eskdale Railway uses both steam and diesel locomotives to pull its coaches

WHITE MOSS COMMON, RYDAL

*B*etween Ambleside and Grasmere, the A591 winds through the heart of Wordsworth country, past Rydal Water and towards the popular viewpoint of White Moss. Here there is parking on the site of a former quarry and access to the White Moss Picnic Site and Nature Trail.

HOW TO GET THERE

Take the A591 from Ambleside, travelling through Rydal and along the northern shore of Rydal Water. As the road leaves the lake, there is parking on either side. The picnic site is well signposted at the entrance to the left, set among trees close to the River Rothay.

FACILITIES

Attractively landscaped car park in old quarry.
Access to wetland common and nature trail (leaflet available).
Toilets and drinking water available.
Facilities for disabled visitors.
Tourist information board.

THE SITE

The White Moss Common picnic area and car park is set on an attractive landscaped site in the heart of the Lake District National Park, on an area of wetland by the River Rothay, which links Rydal Water with Grasmere. The site is owned by the National Trust, and there is parking for about 100 cars.

In addition to the popular ascent

of White Moss (460ft/140m), with its superb views across Grasmere and Rydal Water, the National Trust has provided a circular nature trail through the wetland of White Moss Common, which takes about 20 minutes.

WHAT TO SEE

A range of different habitats can be seen on the nature trail. Crossing the footbridge over the Rothay, you may see white-bibbed dippers feeding under the water. Entering the wetland conservation area, the carr woodland of alder and willow has developed into open glades where water forget-me-nots, valerians and red marsh cinquefoils grow. On the drier ground, birch and aspen flourish, giving shelter for marsh tit, willow warbler and chiffchaff in summer. The fluffy cotton-wool heads of cotton grass which probably gave the common its name are apparent on the wetter ground.

The footpaths beside Rydal Water were often walked by Wordsworth and his family

CLOSE BY

Just 1½ miles (2.5km) north along the A591 is Dove Cottage in the village of Grasmere, where William Wordsworth lived between 1799 and 1813.
(See also page 29.)
Nearby Ambleside is a busy little town.
(See also page 4.)

RYDAL

Hamlet on A591, 1 mile (1.5km) NW of Ambleside

Rydal Mount
Tel: 015394 33002

The Church of St Mary (known as Rydal Chapel) was built in 1824 by Lady Ann Fleming. Wordsworth and his family worshipped at the church and the poet's pew is in front of the pulpit. Behind the church is Dora's Field which Wordsworth gave to his daughter. It is planted with daffodils.

In 1813 William Wordsworth brought his family to Rydal Mount and he stayed here until his death in 1850, drawing inspiration from the wonderful Lakeland views from the house. The family he brought with him included not only his wife and daughter, but his sister Dorothy. However, family life was not all happiness and contentment. Dorothy's protracted descent into mental illness caused him great sorrow, and when his beloved daughter, Dora, died, he was inconsolable. There were, of course, many happy times too, and Wordsworth frequently

Wordsworth's beautiful garden at Rydal Mount

played host to other literary figures, including Samuel Taylor Coleridge and Matthew Arnold.

The house is now owned by a descendant of the poet, and the living rooms and bedrooms which the Wordsworths occupied are on show to visitors, along with the study he built onto the house. The room above the stables, used as a schoolroom for Dora Wordsworth, has a special display and a shop selling books and souvenirs.

All around the house are family portraits, personal possessions and first editions of Wordsworth's work, but his presence is felt most, perhaps, in the lovely gardens which he designed and created himself, and where he would pace up and down, formulating his verse.

Open Mar–Oct daily; Nov–Feb most days. Closed last 2 weeks of Jan.

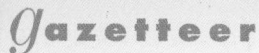

ST BEES
VILLAGE ON B5345, 4 MILES (6.5KM) S OF WHITEHAVEN

The small seaside town is the start of Wainwright's famous Coast-to-Coast Walk (190 miles/304km) to Robin Hood's Bay in North Yorkshire and it also lies on the Cumbria Cycle Way. The Church of St Mary and St Bega has a magnificent Norman doorway. The sandstone cliffs of St Bees Head (462ft/141m) are now a nature reserve with many seabirds, including guillemots, puffins and terns.

SCA FELL AND SCAFELL PIKE
MOUNTAINS W OF LANGDALE

A popular walking and climbing region. Scafell Pike is England's highest mountain at 3,210ft (978m). Most of the range now belongs to the National Trust.

SHAP
SMALL TOWN ON A6, 9 MILES (14.5 KM) S OF PENRITH

The town is famous for its bad weather, as most winters the A6 over Shap summit is blocked by snow. The Shap quarries, which supplied the stone for London's Albert Memorial, are south of the village. Keld Chapel, to the south-west, is preserved by the National Trust. The small building dates from the 15th century and is still occasionally used for services.

Shap Abbey
1½ MILES (2.5KM) W ON BANKS OF RIVER LOWTHER

Right: The ruins of Shap Abbey lie to the west of the village

Far right: Sizergh Castle contains some fine Elizabethan carvings

Shap Abbey (English Heritage) was founded by the Premonstratensian order in 1199, and dedicated to St Mary Magdalene. The abbey was dissolved in 1540 and most of the ruins date from the 13th century, some of which are standing to first floor height. The most impressive feature is the 16th-century west tower of the church.

Open any reasonable time.

The castle has a 60-ft (18-m) high pele tower, built in the 14th century, but most of the castle dates from the 15th to the 18th centuries. There is a Great Hall and some panelled rooms with fine carved overmantles and adze-hewn floors. The gardens were laid out in the 18th century and contain the National Trust's largest limestone rock garden.

Open Apr–Oct, most days.

A crossing point of the River Brathay. Further upstream, Skelwith Force, although only 15ft (4.5m) high, is dramatic after rain. There are workshops and a slate showroom at Kirkstone Galleries.

The region's third highest peak (3,054ft/931m), Skiddaw is composed of softer rock, containing graphite, than that found in nearby Borrowdale. It is a magnificent climb of just over two hours.

SIZERGH CASTLE
Mansion off A591, 3½ miles (5.5km) S of Kendal
Tel: 015393 60070

SKELWITH BRIDGE
Hamlet on A593, 2 miles (3km) W of Ambleside

SKIDDAW
Mountain 4 miles (6.5km) NW of Keswick

TARN HOWS

Tarn Hows is one of Lakeland's pearls. Its beauty is legendary: still waters reflecting tall stands of firs and larches and rocky islets topped by pines.

Grid ref: SD322998
INFORMATION
The walk is just under 2½ miles (4km) long.
Steep and stony path at first, then level around the lake.
A few wicket gates.
No refreshment facilities near by.
Picnics are possible anywhere, but the grassy slopes and headlands along the south shore are ideal.

START
The walk starts from Glen Mary Bridge on the A593 between Skelwith Bridge and Coniston. There is a small car parking area among the trees on the east side of the road, just south of Glen Mary Bridge and Yew Tree Tarn – look out for National Trust signs 'Tom Gill' and 'Glen Mary' next to the pull-in.

DIRECTIONS
From the car park, cross the stream by the footbridge and turn right, along a stony path. Continue uphill on this path, through oak woodland with the tumbling gill to your right. The path bends round to the left. Several paths appear and disappear up the slope and it is not always easy to follow the right one, but this is not critical: keep heading up with the cleft of the gill just to your right. Eventually the path leads to a wicket gate. After this the ground begins to level off. The series of waterfalls is the Glen Mary Falls. Continue uphill with the stream still on your right. Soon the trees end and the path leads out on to the lake shore. Turn right along the wide track and go through the gate, then simply keep to the smaller gravelled path above the lake shore. The south side of the lake has open grassy places: these give way to birch groves and conifers in Rose Castle Plantation on the east side, whilst the north and west sides are heavily wooded with ornamental plantings of tall conifers. Keep to the main path. (For a challenging detour, a path to the right leads to the ridge of Tom Heights. This is the peak to the west of the lake and offers spectacular panoramic views.) The main path soon leaves the shore, but if you want to explore the marshy inlets there are side-paths which link up eventually with the main path again. Continue along the main path to the starting place just before the gill and the gate, then turn right to follow the path back through the wood.

Old trees, new trees
The trees of the Lakeland valleys were once an important resource, managed in coppices and cut down to their bases every ten

years or so to provide crops of sturdy poles. The poles were then used either to make bobbins in local factories or to make charcoal, the fuel needed to smelt iron. Although they were coppiced regularly the trees were never removed or killed. Trees have stood on this spot for at least 8,000 years. Some, such as the small-leaved limes which grow among the oaks close to the gill, are rare and are only found in ancient woods. The stands of conifers around Tarn Hows were planted in Victorian times

Tarn Hows from Sawrey Viewpoint

WHAT TO LOOK OUT FOR

The pedunculate oak of southern England is replaced in the Lake District by the sessile oak. If you look carefully at the leaves you will see that they taper at the base and have a long stalk, unlike the southern oak which has lobes and a short stalk. Three species of bird – wood warbler, pied flycatcher and redstart – are summer breeding visitors to these woods.

TARN HOWS
LAKE OFF A593, 2 MILES (3KM)
NE OF CONISTON

The lake was bought and sold on to the National Trust by Beatrix Potter. It is a popular beauty spot with magnificent mountain views. (See also Walk on page 76.)

TAYLOR GILL FORCE
WATERFALL 1 MILE (1.5KM)
S OF SEATHWAITE

Two paths lead from Seathwaite to the spectacular 100-ft (30.5-m) waterfall in a steep ravine.

TEMPLE SOWERBY
VILLAGE ON A66, 6 MILES
(9.5KM) NW OF APPLEBY-IN-
WESTMORLAND

The village has a sloping green surrounded by red sandstone Georgian houses, typical of the Eden Valley.

Acorn Bank Garden
N OF TEMPLE SOWERBY, OFF
A66
TEL: 017683 61893

Thirlmere

The small but delightful garden of some 2½ acres (1ha) has a particularly interesting walled kitchen garden. It has been turned into a herb garden with an extensive collection of over 180 varieties of medicinal and culinary herbs. Scented plants are grown in the small greenhouse. A circular walk runs beside Crowdundle Beck and the watermill is open to the public.

Acorn Bank Garden is in the care of the National Trust. Open Apr–Oct, daily.

Thirlmere became Manchester's first Lakeland reservoir when its northern end was dammed, drowning the hamlet of Ambroth and several farms. The A591 runs along the eastern edge of the lake and a minor road skirts its western shores – an attractive drive through woods with forest trails leading off from the car parks. Raven Crag and Hause Point are both good viewpoints.

THIRLMERE

LAKE 4 MILES (6.5KM) SE OF KESWICK OFF A591

Sheep graze the fells near Threlkeld

The hamlet is at the foot of Seat Howe. The Thornthwaite Gallery, set in an attractive 18th-century barn, deals in fine arts.

THORNTHWAITE

HAMLET OFF A66, 3 MILES (5KM) NW OF KESWICK

This quiet village is overlooked by the peak Blencathra. In 1904 one of the first English sanatoria was built for tubercular patients; it is now Blencathra Holiday Centre. The Blencathra Hunt have their kennels here and there is a monument in the churchyard to former members of the hunt. The Threlkeld Sheepdog Trials are held in mid August.

THRELKELD

VILLAGE ON A66, 4 MILES (6.5KM) E OF KESWICK

The Furness Railway reached here in 1859, built to carry stone and slate from the quarries. The Green Cottages, so called because of the colour of the stone, were constructed by the railway company.

TORVER

HAMLET ON A593, 2 MILES (3KM) SW OF CONISTON

TROUTBECK
VILLAGE OFF A5091, 3 MILES (5KM) N OF WINDERMERE

Troutbeck's houses are spread along narrow country lanes

Troutbeck stretches for a mile or so along the hillside without any real centre, an inviting succession of enclaves that consist of large, 17th- and 18th-century yeoman or 'statesman' farmhouses, each with its range of buildings and each centred on a well or spring. In the 19th century infill housing was built. The whole village is a delight in vernacular detail, and the observant eye will find much to feast upon. The buildings are of slate, many bare stone, some rendered and painted. A number have the locally typical conical chimneys. Some houses still have their first floor spinning galleries, some their oak-mullioned windows. In the walls are slate drinking troughs for the horses that used the Kirkstone Pass.

Quite separate from the village is the old school and the church, rebuilt in the 18th century, which has a fine window by Burne-Jones, William Morris and Ford Madox Brown.

Beatrix Potter's 2,000-acre (810-ha) farm, Troutbeck Park Farm, is one of the most famous sheep farms in the Lake District, with three peaks over 2,000ft (608m) high. Her sheep were Herdwicks, tough fell sheep whose wool was traditionally used mainly for rugs. When Beatrix Potter died in 1943 she left the farm and its flock to the National Trust.

Townend
ON S OUTSKIRTS OF TROUTBECK
TEL: 015394 32628

Situated at the southern end of the village is Townend, a farmhouse built in about 1626 by 'statesman' George Browne and remaining in his family until it was acquired by the National Trust. The walls and three massive round chimneys are whitewashed, while the splendid barn with its spinning gallery is unrendered slate. Its interior is exceptionally well preserved, with timbering, stone floors and a large farm kitchen.

ULDALE
VILLAGE OFF B5299, 7 MILES (11KM) S OF WIGTON

An isolated village whose name means 'wolf's dale'. Close by, at Aughertree, are the remains of a Roman camp.

*T*his delightful lakeside walk follows a rocky, undulating path through woods and pastures set below a craggy fellside. The path rounds several picturesque promontories before descending to a landing stage in the Howtown inlet, from where the lake steamer returns you to the start.

The Lady of the Lake

Grid ref: NY390169

INFORMATION

The walk is 7 miles (11km) long. Boots and basic agility are required for the rough paths. Provisions and toilets in Glenridding.
Perfect picnic spots on the rocky lakeside.

START

Glenridding village is on the A592, midway between Penrith and Windermere. Park in the public car park (charge) by the pier, and check return sailing times from Howtown before you set off. Lake steamers operate from Easter to October, but may be cancelled in rough weather (Glenridding Pier, tel: 017684 82229).

DIRECTIONS

Take the lakeside path south from the car park exit. Cross the main road and climb some steps to a path which, despite one more crossing, continues parallel to the road through trees. On pavements now, continue through Patterdale: 100yds (91.5m) beyond the church, turn left on the track to Side Farm.
   Turn left in the farmyard,

Walk

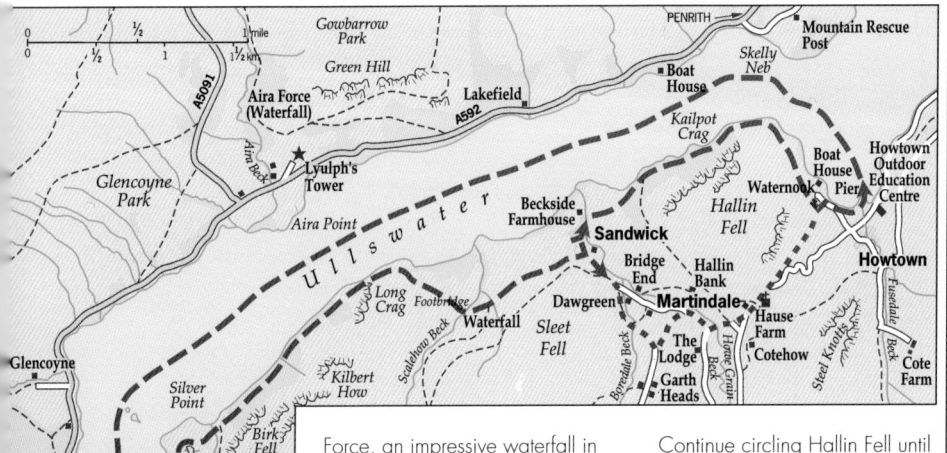

signposted 'Lakeside path to Sandwick and Howtown', and follow a track beneath the rock-studded and bracken-clad fell. Ignore gated tracks forking left and lesser trails bearing off right. Soon the track degenerates into a rough bridleway and brings a thrilling, sudden view of the lake before dipping and rising to Silver Point – an excellent picnic spot. The rocky path undulates through woodland pitched steeply above the shore before veering away from the lake to bring a distant view to the right of Scalehow

Force, an impressive waterfall in spate. Soon after, the path meets a lane: follow this down to the left, into the hamlet of Sandwick. (For an alternative route here, see *below.)

Faced by several gates at the lane end, take the furthest right and cross the beck, heading back to the lake shore. Beyond several field gates, the path creeps over bony tree roots in Hallinhag Wood to emerge at Geordie's Crag, another fine viewpoint. Children can be supervised as they explore the landward-facing rocks here, but keep them away from a dangerous slope overlooking the lake.

Continue circling Hallin Fell until 50yds (45m) beyond Waternook. Turn left here through a wall gate and descend steps to the shore of Howtown inlet. Follow the lakeside path and cross the footbridge to Howtown Pier, to catch the steamer back to Glenridding.

*Alternatively, turn right in Sandwick and follow the lane towards Martindale House and Boredale. At the junction turn sharp left, back towards Hallin Fell. Continue and keep left, to pass Martindale church on the right. Turn left just after the church on to a grassy track, to meet the main route at the wall gate.

WHAT TO LOOK OUT FOR

Spared the bustle of Windermere, and flanked by attractive fells, Ullswater is the more peaceful and picturesque of the two largest stretches of water in the Lake District. The two steamers, Lady of the Lake and Raven, were built more than a hundred years ago and converted to run on diesel oil in the 1930s.

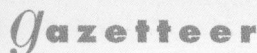

ULLSWATER
LAKE ON A592, N OF PATTERDALE

Ullswater is the second largest lake in the Lake District, 7 miles (11km) long. The northern and western shorelines are National Trust owned. Often considered one of the most beautiful lakes, its setting is spectacular, in a steep glaciated valley. Cruisers serve the length of the lake from Glenridding to Pooley Bridge and Howtown.

(See also Walk: Discovering Ullswater, page 82.)

ULPHA
VILLAGE OFF A593, 4 MILES (6.5KM) N OF BROUGHTON-IN-FURNESS

A pleasant village near the River Duddon. The church was restored in the 19th century but the 16th-century east window remains.

ULVERSTON
TOWN ON A590, 8 MILES (13KM) NE OF BARROW-IN-FURNESS

This pleasant market town with old buildings, cobbled streets and alleys, is linked to the Leven Estuary by England's shortest ship canal. On Hoad Hill stands a monument to Sir John Barrow, founder of the Royal Geographic Society.

Conishead Priory
PRIORY ROAD SE OF ULVERSTON

A Victorian Gothic mansion stands today on the site of a medieval Augustinian priory. Now a major Buddhist centre, and under restoration, it has fine plaster ceilings, stained-glass windows, a cantilever staircase, a vaulted hall and cloister. A private woodland walk leads to Morecambe Bay.

Open Etr–Sep, most wknds & BHs, afternoons only.

Laurel & Hardy Museum
4C UPPER BROOK ST
TEL: 01229 582292 & 861614

Ulverston was the birthplace of Stan Laurel, so perhaps it is not surprising that the town should boast the world's only Laurel and Hardy Museum, now extended to more than double the original floor area. Exhibits include a display of Oliver Hardy memorabilia obtained from Harlem, Georgia (Ollie's birthplace), and wax figures of Laurel and Hardy from the House of Wax at Great Yarmouth. Newsreels and documentary films are shown continuously, and hourly talks given on Laurel and Hardy.

Open all year, daily.

Left: The memorial cross in Ulverston's market place

Below: Boats for hire on Ullswater

UNDERBARROW
VILLAGE OFF B5284, 3 MILES (5KM) W OF KENDAL

A farming village, with a mild climate, which has won the Best Kept Village award on several occasions.

WASDALE HEAD
HAMLET ON MINOR ROAD, OFF A595, N OF WAST WATER

A small welcoming hamlet where British rock-climbing began in the 1880s, it is now a climbing centre for the local high peaks. The church, believed to be the smallest in the country, is hidden in a tiny copse of trees. Looking like a small barn, it has a tiny window with the appropriate inscription 'I will lift up mine eyes unto the hills'.

gazetteer

Left: A classic view of Wast Water
Below:A bridge spans the beck at Watendlath

The deepest lake in England (260ft/79m) and surrounded by wild, rugged countryside, Wast Water is an important habitat for crustacea and unusual plants. It is bounded on the south-east by impressive scree slopes. The view to the peaks at the head of the valley – Yewbarrow, Great Gable and Lingmell – is the National Park logo.

WAST WATER
LAKE ON MINOR ROAD OFF A595, 3 MILES (5KM) NE OF SANTON BRIDGE

An ancient village which now belongs to the National Trust in a picturesque valley south of Derwent Water, on the slopes of High Seat. Watendlath is a popular beauty spot. Sir Hugh Walpole used the village as a setting in his novel *Rogue Herries*.

WATENDLATH
HAMLET OFF B5289, 3 MILES (5KM) NE OF SEATOLLER

This pleasant hamlet is situated at the foot of the Whicham Valley. The small dales chapel has a plain Norman doorway. North of the village is the bulk of Black Combe.

WHICHAM
HAMLET ON A595, 3 MILES (5KM) NW OF MILLOM

WHINLATTER PASS
MOUNTAIN PASS ON B5292, W OF PORTINSCALE

This steep scenic road has excellent views at the eastern end over Bassenthwaite Lake to Skiddaw. Whinlatter visitor centre has exhibitions and forest trails.

WHITEHAVEN
TOWN OFF A595, 7 MILES (11KM) S OF WORKINGTON

A seaside port situated on the west Cumbrian coast, Whitehaven was the first post-Renaissance planned town in Britain, often referred to as the 'Georgian port' due to its wealth of 18th-century architecture. Although much of the town centre has been rebuilt, the remaining 17th- and 18th-century buildings are now Listed. The town was owned at this time by the Lowther family, who also owned the surrounding mines.

Overlooking the harbour on West Strand is The Beacon which houses a sophisticated weather station and introduces visitors to the town's origins and history. The harbour is now a conservation area, and the port is still busy with the fishing fleet and small pleasure boats. West Pier was built by Scottish engineer Sir John Rennie. Along South Harbour are monuments to the mining industry such as the Candlestick Chimney, the mine bogeys and the winding wheel. The last mine closed in 1986.

In the mid-18th century the port of Whitehaven was larger than Liverpool. Its prosperity grew through the export of coal and the import of tobacco and rum from North America. Cumberland rum butter remains a popular local delicacy. George Washington's grandmother, Mildred Warner Gale, lived in Whitehaven and is buried in St Nicholas Gardens.

Sturdy fishing boats at Whitehaven's harbour

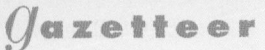
WINDERMERE

TOWN AND LAKE ON A591, 7 MILES (11KM) NW OF KENDAL

The confusion of names between the town and the lake stems from the days when the Kendal and Windermere Railway Company was opened in 1847. Its terminal station was at the village of Birthwaite, hardly a name to bring tourists flocking in, so the railway company changed the name of the station to Windermere, even though it is 1 mile (1.5km) from the lake. A footpath opposite the railway station and beside the Windermere Hotel leads through the woods to the top of Orrest Head, a 784-ft (239-m) hill north of the town, to one of the finest views in Lakeland.

The town quickly developed around the station, filled with hotels, boarding houses and shops, and spread down the hill towards the village of Bowness on the lakeside. These days Bowness has taken over as the tourist centre, but Windermere remains a busy town.

Gazetteer

Left: Windermere from Gummers How

Below: A steam kettle on the Osprey at Windermere Steam Boat Museum

Windermere, the lake, is the largest in England, being 10½ miles (17km) long and about 1 mile (1.5km) wide at its broadest point. It can be crossed by ferry from Bowness to Far Sawrey, or by passenger boat between Lakeside, Bowness and Ambleside.

This unique and historic collection of Victorian and Edwardian steamboats and vintage motorboats reflects the enormous part boating has played over many years in the history of lake Windermere – a popular lake for both motorboat and sailboat enthusiasts. Many of the exhibits in this extensive collection are still afloat and in working order, including the oldest steamboat in the world – the S L *Dolly* of 1850. Displays tell the social and commercial history of the lake.

Open Mar–Oct, daily. Steam boat trips weather permitting.

Windermere Steam Boat Museum
RAYRIGG RD
N OF BOWNESS BAY
TEL: *015394 45565*

WINSTER
VILLAGE ON A5074, 3 MILES (5KM) S OF WINDERMERE

An unspoilt, scattered village of whitewashed stone cottages. The River Winster, which formed the border between Westmorland and Lancashire, flows through the centre.

WITHERSLACK
HAMLET OFF A590, 3 MILES (4.5KM) N OF LINDALE

A tranquil village where, until the mid-19th century, the Earls of Derby held manor courts at the Derby Arms inn.

WORKINGTON
TOWN ON A597, 17 MILES (27KM) W OF KESWICK

The town is situated at the mouth of the River Derwent and the harbour is home to the Vanguard Sailing Club. Workington Hall, now demolished, was built in 1379, and Mary Stuart stayed here when fleeing to England in 1568.

Helena Thompson Museum
PARK END RD
TEL: 01900 62598

Costumes, glass, ceramics and other decorative arts and objects of local historical interest form the core of exhibits in this small museum in Workington. The items are displayed in a pleasant 18th-century house, and temporary exhibitions are shown in the former stable block.
  Open all year, most days.

WRYNOSE PASS
MOUNTAIN PASS OFF A593, ON MINOR ROAD TO ESKDALE GREEN

One of the most dramatic roads in the Lake District, the summit of the pass is 1,281ft (391m) high. The steep road can get very crowded in summer.

The narrow road climbs steeply up Wrynose Pass

LISTINGS

USEFUL ADDRESSES AND NUMBERS

The Forest Enterprise Centre, Grizedale
Tel: 01229 860010

Lake District National Park Visitor Centre, Brockhole
Tel: 015394 46601

Lake District Weather Service
Tel: 017687 75757

National Park Information Centre, Keswick
Tel: 017687 72803

Travel Link
Tel: 01228 606000

Whinlatter Visitor Centre, Braithwaite
Tel: 017687 78469

There are National Trust Information Centres at:
Bridge House, Ambleside; Lakeside; Keswick; The
Square, Hawkeshead; Wordsworth House,
Cockermouth; Fell Foot Country Park, Newby
Bridge.
Tel: 015395 31273 or 015394 35599
(Grasmere)

TOURIST INFORMATION CENTRES

Alston, Alston Railway Station
Tel: 01434 381696

Ambleside, The Old Courthouse, Church Street
Tel: 015394 32582

Appleby-in-Westmorland, Moot Hall, Boroughgate
Tel: 017683 51177

Barrow-in-Furness, Forum 28, Duke Street
Tel: 01229 870156

Bowness-on-Windermere*, Glebe Road,
Bowness Bay
Tel: 015394 42895

Cockermouth, The Town Hall
Tel: 01900 822634

Coniston*, Ruskin Avenue
Tel: 015394 41533

Egremont, Lowes Court Gallery
12 Main Street
Tel: 01946 820693

Forton, M6 Service Area,
Tel: 01524 792181

Grange-over-Sands, Victoria Hall, Main Street
Tel: 015395 34026

Grasmere*, Red Bank Road
Tel: 015394 35245

93

Hawkshead*, Main Car Park
Tel: 015394 36525

Kendal, Town Hall, Highgate
Tel: 01539 725758

Keswick, Moot Hall, Market Square
Tel: 017687 72645

Killington Lake, Road Chef Service Area M6
(southbound), nr Kendall
Tel: 015396 20138

Kirkby Lonsdale, 24 Main Street
Tel: 015242 71437
(Limited winter opening)

Kirkby Stephen, Market Square
Tel: 017683 71199
(Limited winter opening)

Maryport, Maryport Maritime Museum,
1 Senhouse Street
Tel: 01900 813738

Penrith, Penrith Museum, Middlegate
Tel: 01768 867466

Pooley Bridge, The Square
Tel: 017684 86530

Seatoller, Seatoller Barn
Tel: 017687 77294

Sellafield, Sellafield Visitors Centre, Seascale
Tel: 019467 76510

Southwaite, M6 Service Area
Tel: 016974 73445/6

Ullswater*, Main Car Park, Glenridding
Tel: 017684 82414

Ulverston, Coronation Hall, County Square
Tel: 01229 587120

Waterhead*, Car Park, Ambleside
Tel: 015394 32729

Whitehaven, Market Hall, Market Place
Tel: 01946 695678

Windermere, Victoria Street
Tel: 015394 46499

*Denotes seasonal opening only

INDEX

Abbot Hall Art Gallery, Kendal 39
Abbot Hall Museum of Lakeland Life and Industry,
    Kendal 39
Acorn Bank Garden, Temple Sowerby 78
Aira Force 5
Ambleside 5
Appleby-in-Westmorland 5
Barrow-in-Furness 5
Bassenthwaite 6
Beatrix Potter Gallery, Hawkshead 34
Boot 6
Borrowdale 6
Bouth 7
Bowness-on-Windermere 7
Braithwaite 7
Brantwood, Coniston 16
Brockhole, The Lake District National Park Visitor Centre 8
Brothers Water 8
Brougham Castle 8, 65
Broughton-in-Furness 8
Buttermere 9
Caldbeck 10
Calder Bridge 10
Cars of the Stars Motor Museum, Keswick 40
Cartmel 10
Cockermouth 11, 12–15
Colton 16
Conishead Priory, Ulverston 84
Coniston 16
Coniston Water 18
Crook 18
Crosthwaite 18
Crummock Water 18
Dacre 18
Dalemain, Dacre 19
Dean 15
Derwent Water 20
Dove Cottage & Wordsworth Museum, Grasmere 29
Dunnerdale 21
Eaglesfield 15
Eden Valley 22–3
Edenhall 23
Egremont 24
Elterwater 24

Ennerdale Water 25
Eskdale 25
Esthwaite Water 25
Field Broughton 25
Finsthwaite 26
Furness 26
Furness Abbey, Barrow-in-Furness 5
Glenridding 26
Gosforth 26
Grange 26
Grange-over-Sands 26
Grasmere 28
Great Gable 32
Grizedale Forest 33
Hardknott Pass, 34
Haverthwaite 34
Haweswater 34
Hawkshead 34, 35–7
Helena Thompson Museum, Workington 92
Helvellyn 38
Hill Top, Near Sawrey 60
Holker Hall & Gardens 40
Holmbrook 38
Honister Pass 38
Hutton Roof 39
Hutton-in-the-Forest 38
Kendal 39
Kentdale 40
Kentmere 40
Keswick 40
Kirkstone Pass 41
Lake District, The 43
Lakeside & Haverthwaite Railway 52
Langdale Pikes 53
Laurel & Hardy Museum, Ulverston 84
Levens Hall 54
Lingholm Gardens, Keswick 41
Lodre Falls 55
Lorton, Low and High 56
Loweswater 15, 56
Lowther 56, 65
Maryport 56
Millom 56
Mirehouse, Keswick 41

INDEX

Muncaster 57, 58–9
Mungrisdale 57
Near Sawrey and Far Sawrey 60
Newby Bridge 61
Patterdale 61
Penrith 62–5, 66
Pooley Bridge 65, 67
Ravenglass 67
Ravenglass & Eskdale Railway 68
Rydal 72
Rydal Mount 72
St Bees 74
Sca Fell and Scafell Pike 74
Shap 74
Sizergh Castle 75
Skelwith Bridge 75
Skiddaw 75
Steam Yacht *Gondola*, Coniston 17
Tarn Hows 76–8
Taylor Gill Force 78
Temple Sowerby 78
Theatre in the Forest, Grizedale Forest 33
Thirlmere 79
Thornthwaite 79

Threlkeld 79
Torver 79
Townend, Troutbeck 80
Troutbeck 80
Uldale 80
Ullswater 82–3, 84
Ulpha 84
Ulverston 84
Underbarrow 86
Wasdale Head 86
Wast Water 87
Watendlath 87
Wetheriggs Country Pottery 65, 67
Whicham 87
Whinlatter Pass 88
White Moss Common, Rydal 70–71
Whitehaven 88
Windermere 90
Winster 92
Witherslack 92
Wordsworth and the Lakeland Poets 30–31
Wordsworth House, Cockermouth 11
Workington 92
Wrynose Pass 92

ACKNOWLEDGEMENTS

The Automobile Association wishes to thank the following photographers and libraries for their assistance in the preparation of this book.

THE MANSELL COLLECTION 30, 31b
SPECTRUM COLOUR LIBRARY 26/7, 32/3, 43, 60/1, 61, 64, 80/1, 85, 92.

The remaining photographs are held in the Association's own library (AA PHOTO LIBRARY) and were taken by A Baker 7, 47, 71, 84/5, 87; Ted Bowness 6, 24/5, 29b, 33, 35, 36, 37b, 48, 57, 72/3, 88/9, 91; S Day 8/9, 16/7, 18/9, 20/1, 29a, 31a, 51, 70, 90/1; A Hopkins 22, 23, 59; S King 25, 37a, 64, 74, 82; C Lees 12, 52/3, 86/7; P Sharpe 10/11, 14/5, 38, 41, 44, 54/5, 63, 65, 66/7, 69, 75, 77, 79; R Surman 15

Cover photographs

EDMUND NÄGELE FRPS: front – main, back – middle
Ted Bowness: back – top and bottom
J A Tims: front (walkers)